CONTENTS

Prelude 1

Introduction (by Fudge) 3

Chapter 1: Born this way 5

Chapter 2: We are family 11

Chapter 3: So good to me 15

Chapter 4: Broken 19

Chapter 5: Let her go 23

Chapter 6: Youngblood 27

Chapter 7: Love changes everything 31

Chapter 8: Anywhere 35

Chapter 9: Harder better faster stronger 41

Chapter 10: Open season 47

Chapter 11: High hopes 53

Chapter 12: King of my castle 57

Chapter 13: Express yourself 61

Chapter 14: Better together 67

Chapter 15: Walking with elephants 73

Chapter 16: Magic 77

Chapter 17: Nothings gonna stop us now 83

Chapter 18: Lovely day 91

Chapter 19: Everywhere 97

Chapter 20: I'll be there 103

Chapter 21: Uptown funk 107

Chapter 22: Slave to love 111

Chapter 23: Holiday 117

Chapter 24: Celebration 123

Chapter 25: One last time 129

Chapter 26: (I've had) the time of my life 137

Epilogue: A quarter past midnight 139

Appendix 1: The miracle that is Fudge Jenkins 144

Appendix 2: Nothing will change my love for you 148

Appendix 3: The Greatest 149

Appendix 4: Starboy 151

Appendix 5: Find me 153

Appendix 6: I miss you 155

Appendix 7: Facebook 156

Appendix 8: No words 157

Appendix 9: I guess I'll wait another lifetime 159

Additional photographs 161

Song titles 167

The Adventures of Fudge Jenkins

Parisa Jenkins

Copyright © 2018 by **Parisa Jenkins**

All rights reserved. No part of this publication may be reproduced, distributed or transmitted in any form or by any means, without prior written permission.

Parisa Jenkins
www.parisajenkins.co.uk

The Adventures of Fudge JenkinsParisa Jenkins. -- 1st ed.
ISBN 9781729444245

Acknowledgements

I would like to say thank you to so many people for the part they played in Fudge's life. If you met him, if you interacted with him positively, if you sent positive thoughts his way then, thank you.

In no particular order, thank you specifically to:

Lisa Lusty, Louisa Blume, June Jeffrey, Sheila Burns, Hannah Davidson, Ashe Littler, Cazzy Govier, James Nicholson, Richard Thornley, Cat's Protection League St Albans, Last Chance Hotel, Rebecca Griffiths, Rebekah Miller, Kerry Smith, Alex Wilson, Hannah Davidson, PDSA Plymouth, Herts Advertiser, Newquay Voice, Maxine Young, Tanya Bedford, Trish Owen, Nadine Littley, Billy Roberts, Deborah Grant, Louise Lawrence, Claire Bailey, Lorna Faulkner, Marion Gould, Kerry Smith, Sarah Everett, Denise and Roger Jenkins, Jo Lutey, Stephen Nixon, Rebecca Gilbody, Riko James Langton, Barbara Walsh, Cheryl Capeling, Rosie Capeling, Cheryl Dee, Jake Phillips, my husband Craig, and our three children Aaron Emily and Kayan.

Finally, thank you to Fleur Churchill for her photographs, Joanna Pearce for her help writing my synopsis and Anna-Lisa Hasedžić of The Globeflower Agency for helping me to edit and publish my book.

Prelude

This book has been written from the perspective of our family cat, Fudge Jenkins. It documents his incredible life and outlines his epic adventures. I sadly wasn't around for his whole life and therefore I have had to write the early chapters with the use of information provided via third parties.

The book has been written as if Fudge was putting pen to paper himself; something that I'm sure if we had challenged him to do he would have somehow managed. I've crafted it to the best of my ability; I hope I've done him proud.

I haven't really had much opportunity to project too much of myself into the book and so, in an impromptu and somewhat geeky act of selfishness, I have retrospectively injected a bit of me into each chapter. Every one of the chapters in this book are named using either song titles or lyrics and, within the body of each chapter, in italics, I have incorporated lyrics from those very songs. Every moment in Fudge's life has had an appropriate song or lyric to emphasise the feelings and the emotions of that particular time because music is, of course, the soundtrack to life. Let's do this.

Introduction (by Fudge)

My name is Fudge Jenkins. I am a cat, a *Siamese* cross, of approximately eighteen years of age. I am not entirely sure what I am crossed with, but, due to my size, colour, and wicked personality, I think it may be *Havana*.

I have a slightly weird and wonderful life for a cat and the entertainment afforded to those who are privileged enough to hear about or experience it is immeasurable. If I was a human, I think I would probably be worthy of my own TV show but, I am not, and I don't have one.

This book has been written outlining most of my adventures and escapades due to popular demand. Quite simply put, it's the 'time of my life' and therefore has the mandatory basics of any story; a beginning, middle, and an end. I do hope you enjoy hearing about my journey, which I have written with the help of my most attentive human slave.

Chapter 1

Born this way

I was born in the year 2000 in a 1930s terraced house in the city of Bath, near Bristol. My first experience of humans was a middle-aged lady who owned and lived in the house where I was born. She cared for me and my other catty companions and was an intriguing, mystical, and eccentric being. Her hands were furnished with an impressive scattering of rings. She had more rings than fingers and I very much thought it must have been quite an effort to dress her fingers every day with such a large amount of hand jewellery. The weight of her hands sporting a variety of different coloured metals and stones must have been considerable. Her nature was, however, far from heavy handed. She was quite the opposite: a kind, gentle, gypsy lady.

The house we lived in was quite small, it had two bedrooms upstairs, one of which was inhabited entirely by cats. The other bedroom was the sleeping quarters of our gypsy lady carer. There was a slight over population of felines in our cat bedroom. The litter that I formed part of resided in there as well as several adult female cats including my mother. (No one really knows who my father was, 'a local moggy' was all the information I could grasp on the matter). Our room was quite a loud place to be. As *Siamese* cats, we all liked to chat a lot and had regular singing competitions, particularly at food time when we tried to convince our carer who was the hungriest. The unwritten rule was the louder you were the more food you required. My voice was not the loudest of the bunch and I had to put a lot of effort into my singing, but I exercised my vocal chords regularly in an effort to strengthen and build them up so that, one day, I would have the volume I desired and would be able to get my message across loud and clear.

There were a few litter trays placed appropriately in our room, but I, like some others, rarely chose to use any of them to no real consequence. Our carer cleared up after us and we never got reprimanded for toileting outside the litter trays, whether this was because she could not keep track of who toileted where, or, simply because she didn't mind and enjoyed caring for us, I am not quite sure. Us cats were all waited on hand and foot and didn't want for anything. It was a good start to my life.

I was born this way

Craig and Debra Jenkins were to become my human parents when I was just eight weeks old. They found me via an advert in a local newspaper called *Trade It* and came to view me and my brothers and sisters. Debra, Craig's childhood sweetheart, wanted a cat and I was to be the first of the Jenkins' babies.

There were seven kittens to choose from but Craig quickly picked me out. I don't really know what it was he saw in me that day, but I like to think that my magnetic personality drew him in. The litter was mainly made up of seal points with pure *Siamese* markings, but there were just two chocolate kittens (which is what Debra and Craig wanted) and I was the chosen one at a meagre cost of just £50. I left with them that day and became one of the Jenkins family.

My first journey in a car was a bit strange. I wasn't really sure whether I liked it. The forward motion unsettled my stomach a bit, but I figured that something good was at the end of the journey so didn't kick up a fuss from the confines of the cat carrier that contained me.

I'm on the right track baby

My home environment suddenly changed. I went from having one female carer, six other siblings, my mother (a seal point *Siamese*) and various aunties to just two humans. This was a bit strange for me initially, but I warmed to Debra and Craig as my new companions. It was nice to have a small family unit where the focus was entirely on me.

The modern detached house in the small suburban village of Severn Beach in Bristol was different to my previous house; there were smaller rooms, but more of them and, initially, no other feline company. The floor space that I had access to was larger than I had previously known and I quickly became king of my new kingdom. I was allowed to roam the entire house rather than be predominantly confined to one room. How magnificent. Eventually, I was allowed outside and this really was a whole new world to me where I developed impressive hunting and fighting skills.

Debra and Craig loved each other, very much, that was, undeniable, and easy for anyone to see or feel. They poured their love into each other and me. I lived like a spoilt child. My vocal efforts sounded louder in my new home, probably due to the fact I had no competition and I had put in so much practice whilst living in Bath. I gave regular impressive vocal demands for food and fresh water drinks, which worked a treat. My needs were constantly met and I took full advantage of my new willing human slaves.

I slept in the family bed, received countless cuddles and kisses from them both, and got fed handsomely. Both Debra and Craig treated me as their much-loved own; I was, after all, their first little baby.

Craig bought me a cat climbing tower with various toys hanging off it as well as a sleeping compartment midway up. I was more impressed with the cardboard box that it came in and spent quite a lot of time exploring and chewing that with my tiny kitty teeth. I didn't think much of the climbing tower at all and despite Craig putting me on it a couple of times to try and encourage me to play on it, it didn't interest me in the slightest. It was boring. I quickly jumped down off it and went back to my cardboard box. I never once showed interest in the climbing tower and was sure to give it a wide berth whenever I had to pass it. It became an item of unused furniture in the house and the only interaction it had was when Debra dusted it on a weekly basis.

Fairly quickly in my new home environment, it became obvious that I had slight digestive problems (as well as an attitude problem) when it came to using the litter tray. I struggled with restraint when it came to calls of nature and Craig became very conscious of my use of any area inside the house as my personal toilet depending where I was when the urge arose. Sometimes my urge was urgent, other times if I felt like going to the toilet somewhere new then I would.

To my surprise toileting in the house in areas other than the litter tray seemed to cause annoyance for my new humans; I didn't really understand why, to be honest. It hadn't been a problem in my previous home.

My tummy troubles resulted in me becoming a case study in an episode on TV with the famous female Norwegian vet Trude Mostue to, unfortunately, no real avail but, I like to think my journey to international stardom started at a very early age.

We are all born superstars

Trude diagnosed me as having an allergy to fish, so, to my annoyance and inconvenience, fish was removed from my daily diet. Fish is actually one of my most favourite things to eat, although, admittedly, some types of fish do not sit well in my stomach.

Once I returned home from my meeting with Trude, I continued to infrequently use the litter tray. As King Fudge (treated like royalty by my humans) I would toilet where I wished.

When I was caught in the act of relieving myself somewhere inside other than the litter tray it resulted in me being, uncompromisingly, exited (at pace) from the house which I guess, was for the purpose of encouraging me to use the outside space as my toilet.

I never really did consider outside or the litter tray as convenient places to toilet so when I did eventually get let back into the house environment I would almost immediately use my regular chosen unorthodox inside toileting area again.

I did learn to become subtler when relieving myself in the house. This subtle or sneaky tactic would delay the temporary evictions that would inevitably follow.

My outside time was mainly spent duelling with neighbouring cats. We had developed a mutual hatred for each other and would illustrate this by regular acts of public fighting. I liked to try win fights by being exceptionally loud during my battles. Win by intimidation or by totally freaking them out; that was my motto. I used (my now impressive vocal chords) to their maximum. All it took, with some of my opponents, was a personal recital of my particularly aggressive fighting song 'I'm going to KILL you,' in my loudest voice and they would run off with their tail between their legs. That wasn't always the case though and I did have to develop my physical battle skills over time to keep myself respected in the local neighbourhood.

I was born to be brave

After a year or so my humans decided to extend their fur baby collection. Smokey and Snowy joined the Jenkins household. They, too, were *Siamese*. In fact, they were my half-brother and sister from the same gypsy lady carer in Bath.

My objection to them was initially obvious. They had invaded my kingdom and I was very LOUD and BIG about my dissatisfaction. I did, however, warm to them within a short time. It actually was nice to have some of the same species around again, although their personalities were massively different than mine.

Snowy was beautiful – I mean utterly beautiful; she was a seal point Siamese and, admirably slender with deep blue eyes that were mesmerising. Her personality, however, was self-centred and selfish. She could be affectionate, but only when it was to her benefit. I learned to accept that about her and quickly provided for her in many ways.

Smokey was, as his name suggests, a smokey colour. He was an amazing being; a cuddle bum with fur like silk. He only ever wanted cuddles and love and that was what he got. Interestingly Snowy and Smokey did like the dust free cat climbing tower that Craig had bought for me and spent time playing on it together. I watched on in disgust. My cardboard box had long been thrown away; what was I supposed to play with now?

Chapter 2

We are family

Life continued in the Jenkins' household in a harmonious family bliss, with me and my two siblings being treated really as Craig and Debra's own babies. We were all incredibly well looked after and despite Craig's occasion dissatisfaction with my toilet habits in the house, all three of us were showered with love and affection from both humans. With my incredible voice I would loudly demand my food at meal times and my siblings chose to accompany me in song with their slightly quieter voices.

Get up everybody and sing

I also took to sitting on the side of the sink on occasion to recite my 'I'm thirsty' song as I developed a palate for fresh water straight from the tap. This proved a successful tactic. Craig or Debra would, eventually, tire of my song and come and turn the tap on so I could drink until I was satisfied. Sometimes it did take longer than I would like for service, but, one of my finer qualities is persistence and my song would not finish until they gave me what I asked for.

This harmonious family-life continued without interruption for a few years and it was a happy content household of perfection. Then, in January of the year 2004, something changed.

Smokey, Snowy and I had the noise level of the household at a manageable level (well, arguably, at meal time, perhaps it exceeded this, as far as the humans were concerned) but, Siamese is a vocal breed and, generally, in my opinion it was a 'satisfactory' noise level for a household with a moderate Siamese population. It was still a lot quieter than my first home in Bath had been.

One chilly winter day something came into the house that was, as far as I was concerned, not welcome; it was exceedingly loud and very demanding of my humans' attention. I later came to learn that this was Debra and Craig's first-born son, Aaron.

Craig and Debbie became much less attentive to us fur babies, not because they loved us any less but because this Aaron was exceptionally time-consuming. He was far from self-sufficient, like us cats. This didn't seem to make Craig or Debbie unhappy, in fact it was quite the opposite, they seemed even more in love now that they had a human baby of their own.

Aaron was, however, not a particularly well child and, there were moments of struggle when it came to deciding what to do about his illness. The three of them spent a lot of time away from the house, returning tired and stressed. I now understand these were journeys to doctors and hospitals in an effort to help Aaron be well. Us cats were left (not neglected in any way) to our own devices to entertain ourselves. This was absolutely fine by me as I have always been incredibly independent and a strong being, however, Snowy, and particularly Smokey, seemed to struggle.

The humans became absolutely consumed with caring and worrying about sickly Aaron. He ended up being admitted to hospital and staying there for four long weeks and I heard Craig and Debra talk of Guillain-Barre syndrome which was the doctor's diagnosis. From the tone of their voices and the worry and stress they were experiencing, it was pretty serious.

During this time Smokey became ill, it wasn't noticed immediately by Craig and Debra, they were so wrapped up with worry and stress about

Aaron. This was unfortunate and actually ended up sadly being the end of Smokey, he became so unwell that he died and I know that Craig carries guilt for not noticing and getting him treatment that would have possibly saved his life.

Smokey was loved very much his whole life, but the trauma of Aaron's illness and treatment meant his time with us was cut far too short. He wasn't, unfortunately, as strong and self-sufficient as Snowy and I; we coped being more independent, Smokey sadly didn't.

As a consequence of Smokey's death, Snowy became withdrawn. She clearly grieved for him and she changed. She no longer craved attention from the humans - which actually wasn't overly forthcoming anyway, but I noticed that her interaction levels with them became less frequent and unnecessary as far as she was concerned. I continued to insist on attention from time to time from Craig and Debra, which, sometimes, resulted in affection (when they weren't too tired or stressed) or I would be told by them, 'No, Fudge,' which I understood and accepted.

During Aaron's stay in hospital there was lots of to-ing and fro-ing by Craig and Debbie coupled with an indescribable amount of worry, stress, and tears. However, (unlike Smokey) he fought to see another day and the fraught episode of illness was, eventually, replaced with a loud, happy, and, thankfully, well child.

Domestic bliss eventually returned once the family put the trauma of what Aaron had got through and the loss of Smokey behind them.

No, we don't get depressed

Aaron seemed to like Snowy and me. This small human intrigued me and him and I started to spend quite a lot of time together. For the next two years we became friends, we shared the attention level of the parents on an uneven scale. Aaron got most of the attention, which, again, I accepted without too much complaint.

Snowy did not really want the little human to interact with her and she became dependent on me for warmth, comfort, and strength. She was actually quite a scared cat. Scared of nothing in particular, but she now found life in general quite scary. I felt it was my job to provide for her. Losing her brother affected her quite deeply.

I cuddled up with Snowy regularly. She willingly accepted cuddles from me (but not from the humans). Quite often when she was sleeping, I would go and accompany her; I almost covered her whole body with mine. I was like a personal and physical security blanket for her. She felt safe when I was with her, but she seldom interacted with anyone else.

Just when the noise levels from Aaron seemed to be lessening, in October 2005 another loud human critter joined the household. Her name was Emily and she was, thankfully, a far healthier child and so her arrival was much less traumatic for us all.

We are family

Chapter 3

So good to me

Life was good. Aaron and Emily got slowly bigger and the house seemed to be regularly filled with human friends – both adults and children. It was a house of family happiness.

Every sky will be blue

Snowy and I continued in our kinship. I provided for her as best I could. I kept her warm with cuddles and brought offerings of food (my hunting efforts) back to the house for us to share; she took it for granted that I cared for her but that really didn't bother me, I liked to provide.

Long as you're lovin' me, lovin' me

I loved spending time in the conservatory as it was warm and I could bask in the sunlight. In the evenings when Craig came home from work, it would be family time in front of the television. My usual place of hanging out would be on either Debbie or Craig's lap where I would get copious amounts of attention and love and I would show my appreciation by purring for long periods of time as loud as I could.

There was a trampoline in the back garden which Emily and Aaron liked to spend a lot of time on. There were occasions where I had experiences of the trampoline – it wasn't really something I would choose to do. I found it a bit unsettling gravity wise, however, rather than grumble about it, I adopted a moonwalking movement which got the point across that I didn't want to participate too much. Once I did this moonwalk manoeuvre, I would be carefully placed back on solid ground again. I would show my appreciation to my rescuer by rubbing against their legs and purring loudly.

The family attentively attended to my requests for food and sometimes even shared their human meals when I sang for them - the children were the most generous with sharing their food.

Despite there always being a water bowl next to my feed bowl in the kitchen, I never really considered the water fresh enough, so it became part of my routine to always demand drinks from the sink. The bathroom sink became my preferred location for drinks. I would perch on the edge of it and loudly demand until someone came and served me. Debra was the most regular provider of my fresh water drinks and she did it with love.

I continued to regularly provide toilet efforts inside the house (affectionately known as 'fudge parcels') which did anger Craig from time to time but, although his volume and tone towards me would heighten once he found one of my many house messes, he quickly would get over it and seemed to continue to love me.

I divided my time outside between my hobbies of hunting and fighting with the neighbouring cats. I enjoyed having independent moments but always enjoyed returning back to the family and our home.

I liked to sleep in the day on Craig and Debra's bed – it was my primary choice of sleeping area. In the summer the sun would glare through the bedroom window and create a sun trap in the centre of the bed. Part of my daily routine would be to spend some time sunbathing in this spot at the appropriate time of day.

This harmonious lifestyle continued for four years; we were the original Jenkins' family and our house was a happy one; full of laughter and love. We carried on, we blossomed; it was a blissful time. Mum and dad adored each other and the human children and us cats were happy and content in what was a perfect family moment.

So good to me

We all wanted to stay in that moment forever, but, unfortunately, it wasn't meant to be that way for too long.

Chapter 4

Broken

The human family often went away for a day or two and why not? Craig and Debbie both worked hard, so it was nice for them to have some quality time away from the demands of home and business.

I got the impression that family holidays were an enjoyable experience as they would all come back refreshed and happy. Don't get me wrong, I'm not saying that they weren't happy before they set off on their adventures, but, a change of scenery was obviously beneficial to them. This was food for thought for me, something I would ponder for some years.

Bags were packed with excitement and in-trepidation and there were mutterings of a place called 'London,' a name I had heard before. Our feed bowls were overloaded beyond their comfortable capacity and Snowy and I were left with easy access to outside. We both managed just fine to fend for ourselves for a couple of days; it was something we had done before with no trouble. I enjoyed the independence of being home alone. I was now an accomplished hunter, so I topped up the food supplies with various small bird snacks.

I'm here alone

It would normally be part of my routine, when the whole family was at home, to bring my hunting efforts back to the house to share with Snowy. I would loudly announce my arrival by way of loud yowling. Snowy would come running at my call knowing that it meant that I had food to share with her, whereas Craig and Debra would not be so enthusiastic. On hearing my familiar, 'I have food' song they would, rather meanly I thought, make sure I could not enter the house with my food parcel. The upside of the family being in London meant that, whilst they were away, Snowy and I could enjoy the variety of snacks I captured wherever we wanted to, inside or outside the house, without interruption. I was happy to face any consequences of our indoor midnight feasts when the humans returned from their holiday.

When the humans came back this time things were far different than ever before. No fuss was made regarding the dinner remnants I had left in the conservatory – it was almost like they didn't see it, although I did see Craig clear it up without complaining. This was strange behaviour for him, he would usually have some stern words with me about any mess I made.

Domestic bliss did not ensue and happiness was nowhere to be seen. There was terrible pain and suffering emanating from Debbie. She was no longer able bodied. A stumble whilst walking with Aaron perched on her back when they were away had resulted in a back injury. She was suffering dreadfully physically and everyone felt it.

I feel I can't even breathe

Hospital and doctor visits became frequent again with, this time, Debbie as the patient rather than young Aaron. It seemed no matter what medication or treatment the doctor administered it didn't help heal or ease the pain. In fact, over the course of the next months, her symptoms got progressively worse. She became pretty much bedridden and I spent lots of time with her cuddling and purring, trying my best to help her.

Don't think I can handle this

On 3 May 2010, things went from bad to worse. Debbie, whilst struggling to physically get out of bed in the morning (which had become the norm for the six weeks leading up to that fateful day due to the increasing intensity of pain) suddenly collapsed. Panic followed; the household was frantic.

I scurried out of the house just as the ambulance arrived. The feeling was horrible, heavy concern and physical and emotional pain and something almost indescribable, an ominous feeling.

A kindly family friend collected the children and whisked them away from the scene. I then watched, with concern, as they carefully placed Debra, who was lying on a stretcher, into the ambulance. Little did I know at this time but, that was to be the last memory I had of her, that, and watching Craig (with stress in his face) climbing into his car then speeding off chasing after the blue light that carried the love of his life.

The house felt empty, an eerie emptiness. Snowy and I were left wondering what had just happened and it felt like a lifetime that we were left by ourselves, but it was, in fact, less than a day.

Where do I go from here I'm so lost

When Craig and the kids returned later that evening they brought with them incredible sorrow. Close family members also came to the house and everyone sat in the lounge, silently and sullenly. It didn't feel good.

The awful unbelievable announcement then came, made serenely and sympathetically to the children; Aaron, at just six years old and Emily, at a mere three years of age were told, 'Mummy isn't coming home. She has died.'

Everyone sobbed and the very private grieving process began.

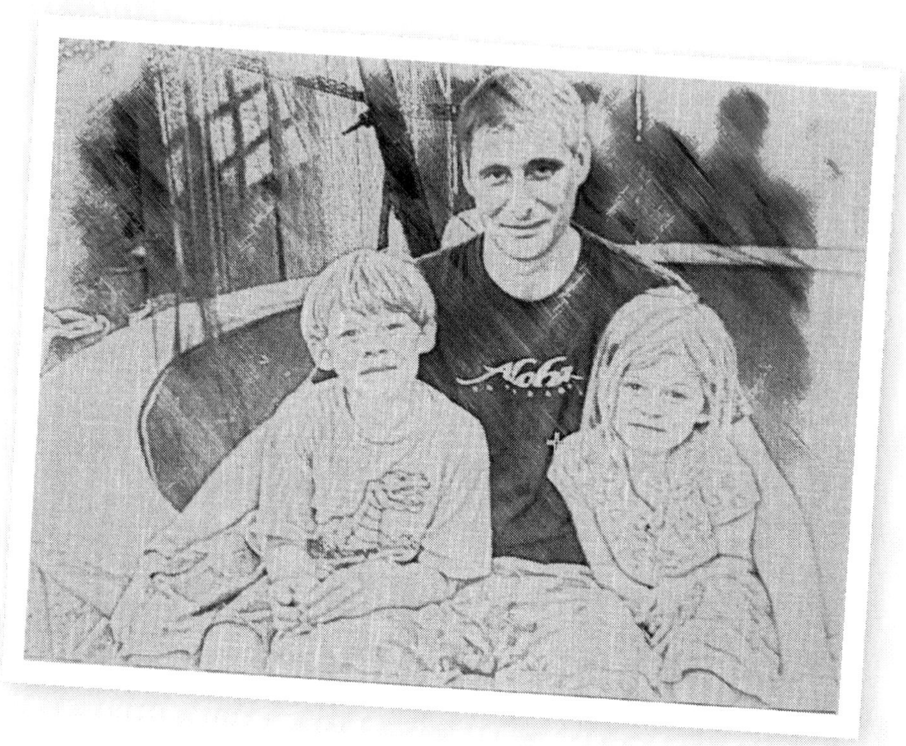
Aloha

Chapter 5

Let her go

The house was empty – not in so much as no one resided there, but, one pivotal and important member of the Jenkins' household was no longer there, and, that changed absolutely everything. It was a depressing atmosphere.

Craig had lost his soul mate, his childhood sweetheart and his best friend and Aaron and Emily (and Snowy and I) had lost our Mummy. Craig sobbed most days and I tried to comfort him with my company and copious amounts of purring. He didn't really want to know or spend time with me at all though and I felt his sadness deeply.

Staring at the bottom of your glass

It was such a sudden loss, so unexpected; one-minute Debra was there and, then, the next moment, the flashing blue light had taken her away never to return to the house again.

The family unit felt broken. It wasn't a fun-loving atmosphere anymore. Craig certainly wasn't the man he used to be, ever the joker always smiling and making fun he had now withdrawn into his shell almost completely. I could see and feel the unbearable suffering he was going through and I think it was coupled with shock. I, too, could honestly not believe that she was gone. There was a strained look in his face and the corners of his mouth seemed to have forgotten what it was to rise and create a smile. The effort of living for him, at that time, was phenomenal. How would he carry on without the love of his life? How would we all carry on without the loving, gentle, kind, caring, wonderful person that was Debra Jenkins?

Staring at the ceiling in the dark

Friends and family rallied round. In terms of physical beings in the Jenkins' home there was a horde of them. People constantly came to the house trying to help lift Craig out of the fog of his dreadful grief and assist him in carrying on with the practical tasks of caring for his and Debbie's children. Everyone continued to try and 'live' however, difficult, or painful, that proved without Debra.

Routines changed in the house. Craig still went off to work, but the to-ing and fro-ing of the kids to school and nursery (which had always been done by Debra) was taken on, and shared by, various family members and friends. Severn Beach was a close-knit community and Craig and Debra were liked by many so had lots of local friends and family who sympathetically helped once they heard of the tragic and unexpected family loss.

The bustling house of Severn Beach was busier than ever in terms of physical beings, but the absence of that one important person made it feel desperately empty and lonely.

Empty feeling in your heart

The bath and bedtime story routine that Debra had adopted over the years for the children was somewhat altered. The kids would still be bundled into the bath, but Craig couldn't seem to do the story time moments – I think it was just too painful for him. It had always been Debra's job to read the children stories at bedtime and Craig just couldn't face doing it. So, the children (and us cats) stayed up later than normal bedtime and we all sat with Craig so that he didn't have to suffer the physical loneliness of being all by himself in the late evenings.

The children seemed surprisingly little affected by the loss of their mum. I don't mean they didn't feel the loss, but their demeanour was very different to Craig's. They appeared relatively happy and seemed to just hold on to Craig at every moment possible. They clung to him with their hearts. Perhaps they were frightened that he too might leave one day and never come back?

Chapter 6

Youngblood

The months passed, the feeling of the household remained low and sullen. It was still a functional household. Craig continued to work hard and family and friends continued their support practically and emotionally. They were, however, all going through the motions in almost a robotic and disbelieving way.

I'm a dead man walking

No one could really come to terms with the fact that she had gone. It was very different. There was a huge void without Debbie. It was the same for everyone. The home and family felt incomplete without her. I missed her motherly cuddles and gentle attentiveness.

Nobody could take my place

I kept expecting her to stroll in and stroke me lovingly from the tip of my nose to the tip of my tail, or, come bounding up the stairs to one of my regular 'I'm thirsty' songs. Craig would, eventually, attend to my calls for fresh water drinks, but not with the enthusiasm, selfless dedication and promptness that Debra had previously afforded. My song therefore became an extended and louder version.

It was a difficult time; there was absolutely no laughter in the house. I continued to receive affection from Craig and the kids, but their hearts weren't in it. I felt that. They were all almost drowning in their own pool of grief. I did personally wonder whether that sad sinking feeling would last forever. It was overwhelming and such a contrast from the previous happy Jenkins family household.

One summer day though, in 2010, some new beings entered our lives. This was the beginning of something new, but for some, it was too much too soon.

But you need it

Grief is a personal struggle and some close family and friends of the original Jenkins' family felt it wasn't the time to introduce anyone new to the family unit. These bystanders too were, of course, struggling to carry their own grief at that time, but, actually, retrospectively, the introduction of new blood into the equation was the start of something really good.

The emotionally low house of Severn Beach in Bristol (the family home that Debra and Craig had poured such love and devotion into) encountered new beginnings in the form of a previously unknown woman and her young son. I wasn't quite sure what to make of them myself, as was the case with many around us.

You're pushing and pushing and I'm pulling away pulling away from you

There was a confidence about them, but not real confidence, I actually think it was strength. A strong woman and her son at that low point in the Jenkins' life had strolled into our home. What was to come of it? Was it right? Was it proper? Did they deserve to be part of our lives? Only time would tell, but I wasn't initially personally convinced.

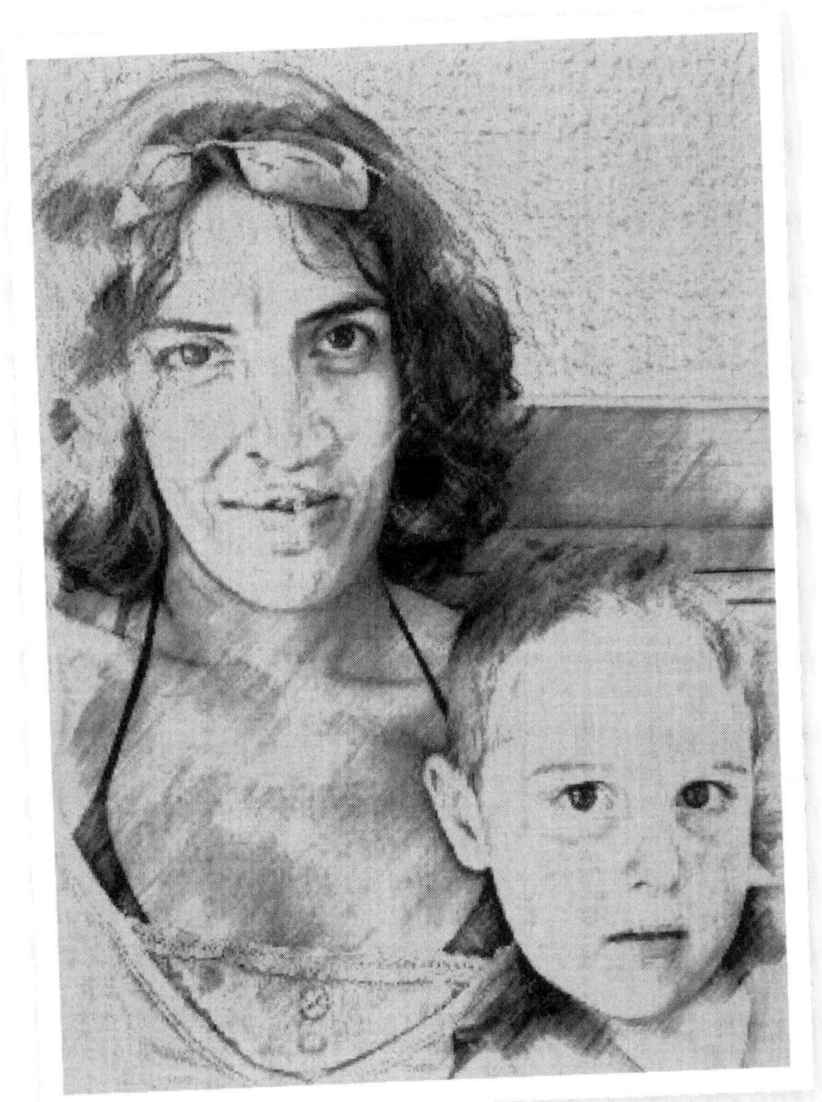

Chapter 7

Love changes everything

The visits from the new people came more frequently, the Jenkins family seemed to enjoy them - it lifted them out of their low feeling. Smiles and laughter returned a little to the house, but the visits from some family and friends became less comfortable and less frequent; they didn't like the new people, not because they were bad people, but more because they were struggling with their own grief and found it hard to accept someone new.

I can't forget her

This perhaps is the right time to properly introduce the new people. *She* seemed to have several variations of name. It took me a while to get the hang of them all. The other being was her three-year old son called Kayan (pronounced 'Kai – Ann').

Kayan called her 'Mummy,' Craig called her 'Prissa' and Aaron, and Emily called her 'Pree- sa.' Other people who attended the house called her 'Pur – iss – a.' She seemed to respond to most names that started with P, but the constant variations were initially difficult to keep up with. I heard her, one day, tell a new friend of the family that she was happy to respond to most variations of her name, but that actually it was spelt P A

R I S A and pronounced like the name Teresa, but with a P instead of a T. The only variation she didn't like was 'Prusilla,' she said.

Parisa had a kindness and firmness about her. She made Craig feel happier and I was pleased with that. I love Craig dearly and it had been so hard to see him so desperately unhappy.

She left I cried for weeks

Kayan was your typical young child, loud, and a bit unruly. He liked me, but had to be reminded by Craig and Parisa to be softer when handling me as he was a bit boisterous – not because he was unkind, but he wasn't really used to handling pets and had to be educated to understand that I was a little more fragile than his teddy bears and needed a gentler hand. I assisted in educating him by growling at him when he squeezed me a bit too tightly, but never needed to use my claws to tell him 'no'. A growl would suffice and he would get the picture fairly quickly. The presence of Parisa and Kayan didn't bother me too much. I'm an adaptable sort. As long as I am fed and loved then I'm a pretty content cat.

I was getting more attention than I had had since Debra had died, but the attention from Parisa was different, more authoritative, more on her terms. My household demands were less pandered to.

Love makes the rules

She, like Craig, didn't like my habit of toileting in the house, but Craig told her in no uncertain terms that there was nothing we could do to change this, he had tried to change this habit of mine for ten years and had finally accepted it was a battle he would never win. Well done Craig.

I was used to demanding loudly for my fresh water drinks and meals when I felt thirsty or hungry and having those 'songs' appreciated and adhered to. Parisa, however, insisted I drink from my water bowl and get fed at designated times of the day. This irritated me slightly.

She ignored my songs, which I thought was quite rude. I think she took the view that I was 'just a cat' and, obviously, this was not the case at all. My preferred title is 'King Fudge' and, in time, she would realise this and acknowledge my status. However, there was to be a considerable effort on my part to bring this to fruition.

I felt hungry and annoyed at times about the new house rules, but nobody seemed to be listening to my demands. The Jenkins' clan were adjusting to a new way, a new start, a new beginning – a much needed light at the end of the tunnel.

Love makes you fly

The atmosphere in the village of Severn Beach changed a bit with many old family friends considering that Parisa did not belong in Craig's life. There was some *ill feeling* towards her, which I considered a little unfair. Although she was enforcing new house rules, she seemed a kind, fair person. I didn't quite agree with their alienation of her, but I understood. It's hard when we lose someone from our life.

Although it had been some months since Debra had died, it clearly still felt like an incredibly short time for many who had been very close to her. I can say, however, from experience that, how someone deals with grief varies from being to being. No one can dictate how long it takes to cope with losing someone close to your heart; it varies for everyone. Craig had carried the burden of his terrible and tragic loss extremely well and had now made the decision to move on. Good for him. Debra was not, unfortunately, coming back, as much as he and anyone may have wished or wanted.

Was I destined to spend my life alone

I saw that Craig was being slightly lifted out of the mist of grief and loneliness by the presence of Parisa and her son. That had to be a good thing, surely?

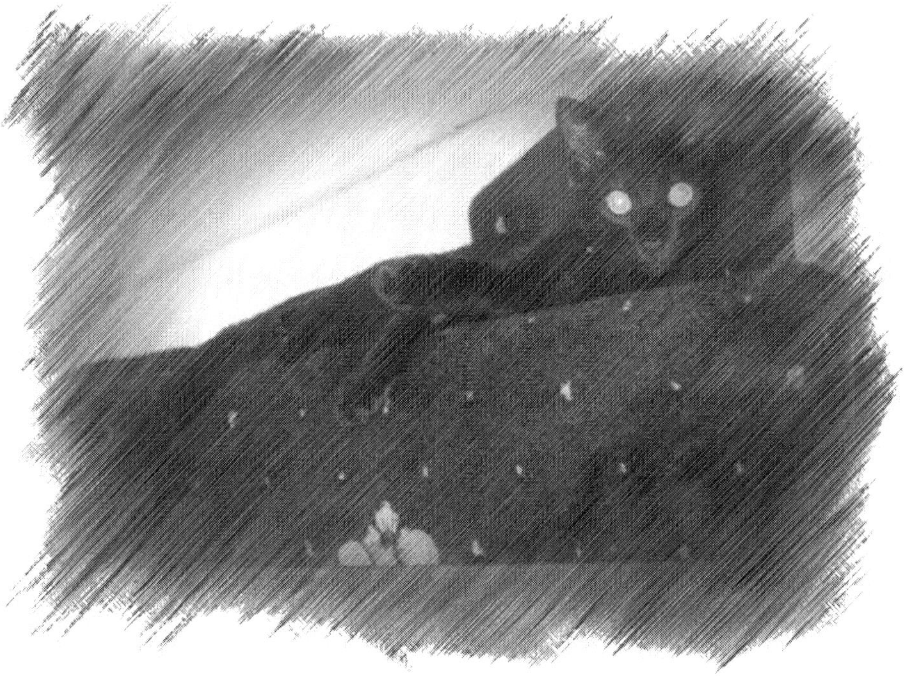

Chapter 8

Anywhere

In September 2010 an additional new-being entered the Jenkins' family home. This one was not human and a far bigger problem for me personally. An energetic eighteen-months-old *Rhodesian Ridgeback* cross dog called Lexi bounded into our home. I immediately considered her my arch enemy and was utterly disgusted and annoyed especially when it became apparent she was moving in on a permanent basis. I made my displeasure known, on introduction and beyond, by my usual behaviour of making myself extremely BIG and LOUD so that everyone understood I wasn't happy.

I continued on a regular basis to make it very clear vocally and physically that I, Fudge Jenkins, was most displeased with my new animal housemate. Funnily enough Snowy didn't seem too bothered by Lexi at all, they both just stayed out of each other's way. I, however, have never been one to take things lying down and the whole family would be reminded by me for many weeks that I was very cross about Lexi's presence.

The attitude of some of the locals remained strained especially once Parisa and Kayan (and troublesome Lexi) moved into Craig's home. Kayan and Emily were enrolled in the local primary school, but this seemed to upset some people and small town syndrome ensued.

When you know that they don't care

Craig made the decision that our time in Severn Beach was up and we promptly moved in November 2010 to a modest 'mansion' in a small rural village called Lower Almondsbury which was less than five miles drive from the previous Severn Beach home.

Oh, I'll go with you anywhere

The three children were enrolled in a new primary school and we started a fresh with reasonable anonymity; a new environment, new people and a new life.

The house was called Hawkfield and was very different to our previous abode. It was an impressive detached Victorian country house surrounded by fields as far as the eye could see with just one visible neighbour who shared the half a mile-long tree-lined driveway off a small country lane.

One of the rooms in Hawkfield was called the Great Hall which had been built by the original owner as a Sunday school church hall. It clearly resembled the space and demeanour of a traditional Victorian church consisting of high ceilings, a vast space, impressive beams, stained glass windows and, overall, magnificence. Nowadays the Great Hall was used as a substantial living room.

Shortly after we moved in Craig bought a grand piano which was housed in the Great Hall and this is when I found out that Parisa was a reasonable pianist and very much appreciated good music. After hours and hours of practice, she managed to play with a reasonable level of competence beautiful modern chart music such as 'Clocks' by Coldplay and 'Cornflake Girl' by Tori Amos on that tremendous piano.

I had never experienced the sound of beautiful music such as that which is generated by a grand piano, so loud that it filled the whole house and if you stood in the large grounds of the garden, you could still feel and hear it ringing through the air. I enjoyed the feeling that the music generated and spent some time perched beside Parisa on the piano stool watching with envy as she played the piano with eloquent joy. It made me feel happy.

Parisa started to warm towards me and would, on occasion, soften to my requests for fresh water drinks straight from the tap and food outside of the scheduled times. No one can resist the charms of Fudge Jenkins.

To somewhere you have never been

The indoor floor space of the property was an incredible 3671 square feet; easily five times the size of our modern home in Severn Beach. There were four bathrooms; two of which were en suite. I had never known such vast luxury. The space available for 'Fudge parcels' was immense and I (almost) never got discovered whilst placing them.

My preferred location for fresh water drinks was the kitchen sink and I learnt to sing for refreshment when someone was in the kitchen as my voice didn't carry well due to the size of the property. If I wanted to be heard I had to make sure someone was in the room otherwise, I could spend literally hours singing in my loudest voice to no effect whatsoever. The outside area was a lash two and a half acre manicured garden with a stable and an abundance of wildlife pickings. I was, honestly, in hunting heaven.

And feel the wind in your hair

My hunting adventures were fun times. There was such an abundance of prey that almost fell into my mouth. It was easy pickings. The offerings I provided to Snowy were, in my opinion, *knighthood worthy*. I would refer to them as 'tremendous' and although that sounds modest, it was true.

There was one particularly impressive hunting escapade that comes to mind. I cunningly and stealthily pursued and captured a rabbit of considerable size and carried the heavy creature up the drive in a cumbersome waddle like fashion. The rabbit, you see, was larger than me and far too much for me to consume by myself and almost too much for me to capture, or carry. I always tried to consider Snowy when hunting anyway, but I was keen on this occasion, not only to share my feast, but to show her how incredible I was to have slain such a large creature. I constantly provided for Snowy at this time. It was, I felt, my responsibility to look after her and this included the provision of food. I cannot think of an occasion where she brought a hunt home for me, although, I know she was capable, and did hunt.

My hatred for Lexi continued; I regularly made a variety of unwelcoming noises at her to remind her not to come too close to me and I made my tail extremely bushy and flattened my ears at every opportunity whilst in her presence in an effort to make her feel as uncomfortable as possible. I composed a song especially for her called, 'I hate you so much right now,' but I never needed to sing it in its entirety to her; she got the message quickly. These methods of mine were very effective in reminding her that I was not fond of her and definitely did not want her anywhere near me.

From afar, however, I did quietly observe her and concluded that she had not been blessed with a sizeable brain.

Darling just look beside you

Generally, Lexi dithered about the house and grounds with her tail mostly swinging from side to side in a rocking horse type motion. I understood the swinging of the tail to mean that (unlike us cats) she was content. She didn't require much to be content. The kids would, when in the garden, throw pine cones for her to retrieve, but although she would chase and get them, she didn't get the concept of retrieving and instead chose to consume them so the children tended to tire of this game quickly; she was a simple creature.

Despite there being a plethora of wildlife in the gardens and surrounding fields of Hawkfield, her hunting efforts were pathetic. She would spot a bird or rabbit then make the decision that this was her hunting moment and bound at it full pelt whilst barking furiously. This method of hers was 100 per cent ineffective when it came to hunting techniques, but it was very comical to observe. She, without fail, always looked surprised that she hadn't managed to catch anything and then, at the next opportunity, would do exactly the same thing all over again. She never seemed to work out that, perhaps, there might be an alternative method that would result in a more successful hunting episode; a simple creature.

Another of Lexi's not so intelligent habits was objecting to the family ever leaving the house. She was, when the family went out, left to roam the gardens, but if she got wind of the family's attempted departure, she would proceed to chase the car down the drive, down the country lane and onto the main road. I think she was trying to say, 'Take me with you,' but the results of these energetic efforts on her part would end in her being brought back to the house in the car and being shut inside which, obviously, was far less fun for her than having the grounds to roam and guard; a simple creature.

The one thing that Lexi was good at was, being a guard dog. Despite not being fierce or aggressive at all, if anyone approached the house when she was outside she would unleash a high volume lengthily barking effort and would not stop until either Craig or Parisa appeared. She sounded very menacing, despite her lack of courage.

I did witness one time a long-time friend of Craig's coming to the house in his car (at a time when Lexi was loose in the garden). She barked relentlessly and fiercely at him and, as the family were not at home, he ended up driving off. What Craig's friend didn't realise is that Lexi wouldn't say boo to a goose so, had he actually got out of the car and walked towards her she would have ran off with her tail between her legs; whimpering. All I had to do was hiss at her and she was gone, brave is not a word to use to describe that dog.

Lexi was so convincing in her guard dog efforts that the neighbours came and complained about her one day. They had attempted to walk the public footpath which went through the fields adjacent to the two properties, on a day that the family were out and Lexi had been left patrolling the garden. She decided that on that day the field too was hers to guard and she barked and barked and chased and chased until they were so frightened that they abandoned their walk and went back into their house. The meek neighbours considered as a result of this experience that Lexi was a fierce and unruly dog. From that day on Lexi no longer got the privilege of roaming the grounds when the family weren't home. She was shut in the kitchen to avoid her tormenting the nervous neighbours. I have always considered dogs as dumb animals, Lexi in my opinion was the definition of stupid. She was definitely a simple creature and I shall, from now on, refer to her by her full name which was 'Stupid Lexi.'

Yeah, I'll go anywhere with you

Chapter 9

Harder better faster stronger

We spent one of each of the seasons living in Hawkfield and every season had a story.

In the autumn the place was covered with a blanket of leaves from the very extensive family of various trees that enveloped the house. Autumn happened to be when I had a near death experience.

The family had been out for the day - they returned later than our normal feeding time and Stupid Lexi was fed before us cats. I was so ravenous that I foolishly thought I would take some dog food from her bowl to take the edge off my hunger. This was a BIG mistake.

As I placed my head in the dog bowl I heard a rumble of a growl and then everything went dark. Stupid Lexi had in a rage of hunger attacked me; she had pierced my neck just shy of an artery and blood had poured out of me knocking me off my feet.

I vaguely remember I was carefully lifted up by Parisa and transported to an animal hospital with mutterings of, 'if we don't take him to the vet, he will die.'

Two days later I had been stitched up and medicated back to reasonable health. I was then transported to what I came to understand to be Craig's parents' house as my family were to go abroad on holiday- something that had been arranged before I got injured.

On my arrival there was lots of wittering from Roger who had a particular aversion for cats, but Denise assured Craig and Parisa that I would be looked after to the best of their ability whilst they were abroad and I watched my family drive away with quiet concern on their faces. They needn't have worried, I was certain I could manage the situation.

I watched intriguingly as Roger carefully made up what seemed to look like a small sleeping area in the garden shed. It looked quite cosy with blankets contained in a generous sized basket. Who on earth was this for? I wondered.

Once I had had my dinner in the kitchen (which I ate enjoyably) I was to my horror, escorted to the shed by Roger. He placed me in the basket and after saying a brief 'goodnight,' then shut the door. This simply would not do and I made my dissatisfaction known with a new song of mine that I made up on the spot called, 'Let me out of here NOW!' There's quite a lot of long howling notes in that song and my volume was quite incredible even if I do say so myself. I was certain that Roger and Denise who were in the house would have heard it along with many of the neighbours.

Work it harder

Aside from the ten minutes that I spent in the shed that night the rest of my seven day stay in Henbury was spent in the house. I slept in the kitchen. Roger, who I knew right from the start didn't like me or the idea of me staying in his home, actually really warmed to me. He fed and chatted to me for most of the time. No one can resist the charms of Fudge Jenkins. He was good company.

Denise was out at work for much of my stay, but the times she was home she was caring and gentle towards me. They both took good care of me tending to my bandages and ensuring I was well, happy and comfortable.

When my family returned from their holiday in Spain I was taken back home with them. I was pretty much back to 100 per cent health then thanks to my foster carers. I acquired a scar as a result of my near death experience in the form of a grey fleck on my neck, which, as the years passed seemed to spread and resembled a poorly fitted bib. This was the first of my nine lives gone.

Make it better

Parisa didn't speak to Stupid Lexi for a whole week after we returned other than to scold her for attacking me; I was starting to realise she really cared for me and I was basking and embracing the added attention and love I was getting from her.

Winter came shortly after and it was cold, a powder white cold. A covering of freezing white stuff engulfed us and my paws became bloody and sore. I left red footprints on the windowsills and slate floor tiles.

The large impressive abode was difficult to keep warm in the cold winter and the family mainly huddled in the small living room with electric heaters blasting at them pretty much constantly when they at were home.

The hunting was harder for me at this time, but I still managed pretty well. Once I had captured a hunting feast, my routine would be to patrol the windowsill of the living room (a large Victorian bay window) and yowl at the top of my lungs my song 'I have food.' This was my announcement to the world that I had been successful in my hunting expedition and my request to my humans that they open the window so I could bring in my food and share it with Snowy. For some unknown reason, they never opened the window for me despite how loud I sang. They would, as a compromise, let me into the outside porch area. After Snowy and I had had our share of the feast, the remnants of my kill would remain there; it became a kind of trophy graveyard.

Do it faster

The white stuff that had covered the grounds and house was called snow and it made a lengthy appearance for us over that winter. Its persistent presence meant that for a few days both Craig and Parisa were unable to leave the property and get to work. They were stranded, much to Stupid Lexi's delight, as their motor vehicles could not defeat the settled snow on the drive and adjoining roads. This made for amazing family time of building snowmen, snowball fights and sledging. The families were bonding together. Good times.

Makes us stronger

Christmas came and the Christian tradition of buying the biggest and fattest turkey for consumption fell upon Craig. He found and purchased a substantial and suitable bird which he foolishly stored on the floor in the detached double garage. The outside temperature was so low that winter that he decided not to store it in the freezer. Silly him. I secretly found it, and, without too much effort, chewed through the packaging making a premature start of eating it. Once Craig discovered my chewings, the whole turkey was placed in the garden for Snowy and I to feed on.

Craig subsequently bought another large (but slightly less magnificent) turkey and stored it more sensibly in the freezer. It was cooked to perfection on Christmas Day and after the humans had had their fill the leftovers were, again, placed in the garden for Snowy and I to have our own Christmas dinner.

More than ever

When spring came, the children embraced the freedom and beauty of the two and a half acre garden and most evenings they would run and play in the gardens without a care in the world. Stupid Lexi followed them around with enthusiasm, her tail swinging from side to side in quiet enjoyment.

With summer came the wondrous invention that is the barbecue. This has to be the best ever human idea. Cooking food on an open fire. I'm good at hunting and providing, but if you can get your meat provided and cooked for you, that really is amazing.

This is how the barbecue goes; humans get meat and then they cook it on the barbecue and it smells and tastes fantastic. Stupid Lexi and I learnt to queue for our barbeque feasts and they were well worth the wait.

Hour after hour

When autumn came again and the prospect of another cold winter rose its icy head, Craig decided we would move on again to not have to shudder through another cold winter.

Work is never over

We moved to Gloucester then; into a nineteenth century gothic cottage in the heart of the city and proceeded into another completely new environment and adventure for all of us.

Chapter 10

Open season

Living in Gloucester was a completely different kettle of fish. The house we moved into was called eight Gothic Cottages in Barton Street in the heart of the busy concrete jungle that is the city centre. It was a small quaint place. I considered that the entire floor space of eight Gothic Cottages could have been accommodated in the vast Great Hall of Hawkfield – it really was a postage stamp in comparison to our previous home. A two-up two-down end terrace house with one downstairs bathroom (which you accessed through the kitchen) and a small courtyard garden in a condensed cul-de-sac off the busy main road of Barton Street. Instead of the views of open fields as far as the eye could see which was what we had enjoyed from the windows of Hawkfield, the scene from Gothic Cottages windows was shops, houses, and heavy traffic.

We were looking out on the greatest view

We crammed into the small space with Kayan and Emily having to share what essentially was a double bedroom separated by a partition. The family was pushed even more together because of the close proximity of the living space.

The city of Gloucester was vibrantly full of people, lots of shops, and lots and lots of traffic. It was the complete opposite to the rural peaceful Hawkfield we had left behind, always noisy, always busy, and, always lots to see and do. I embraced the change and adapted quickly to my new surroundings. I became even more independent with most of my time spent exploring the busy streets of the city.

Now I'm a hundred miles an hour

Eateries were everywhere - no need to hunt - just turn up at a takeaway and demand, loudly; eventually, they gave you food just to get you to go away. Once the proprietors got to know me it got to the stage that I didn't have to demand at all to get food. I would just show up and they knew what I wanted and obliged quickly. I trained them well.

I take it as it comes

I brought some impressive takeaway items home to share and adopted my well-rehearsed 'I have food' song to let everyone know I had been successful in my hunter/gatherer role. My voice seemed quieter in Gloucester probably because I had lots of city noise to compete with so I had to put a lot of effort into singing.

Large joints of pork, entire chicken wings, and legs cooked to perfection were some of my regular takeaway offerings and I heard Craig mutter frequently at my pickings, 'How the hell has he managed to get that? If that hadn't been on the floor or in Fudges' mouth, I would honestly eat that.' He was impressed and envious, understandably, and I felt proud. I ate like a king and my waistline showed it. One day Parisa decided to put me on the scales to see how heavy I was. I weighed in at an impressive fourteen pounds.

The children attended a local primary school and both Craig and Parisa would walk them the mile and a half journey to and from school every day. The morning routine would be most amusing to observe. Initially, there would be a slow exit from the bedrooms by everyone. The adults would encourage the children to get up (shoehorn is an accurate description) then help them get dressed and make sure they all ate a substantial breakfast. Once these tasks were accomplished the whole family would bustle out of the front door and embark on their walk to school.

Before they left, without fail, Parisa would remind everyone to make sure that the kitchen door was left open so that Snowy and I could easily access the litter tray which was kept in the bathroom. This always made me chuckle as, even if I had access to the litter tray, I wouldn't be using it, she should have known that by now.

When Parisa and Craig returned after dropping the kids at school, the kitchen door would always be shut and there would be regular questioning of the children later in the day (to no real avail) about who had managed to not adhere to the rule.

I, for one, knew that it wasn't the children that had shut the door – but they don't listen to me as much as they should. That's been a constant theme in my life.

On two occasions in the space of a few weeks, something else strange happened. One evening, whilst the family were cosying up together in front of the log-burning stove which warmed the sitting room, there was a noise of smashing glass in the kitchen. A wine glass had shattered into unrecognisable slithers in the kitchen sink. Everyone blamed me for this. They thought I had probably been sat on the sink considering starting my rendition of one of my 'I'm thirsty' song and had, inadvertently and clumsily, knocked it over then fled the scene to avoid being told off. They were wrong though. At the time, I had been curled up asleep on Parisa and Craig's bed upstairs. The sound of smashing glass had abruptly woken me, but I definitely wasn't responsible for breaking it.

Two weeks later another wine glass shattered into a million pieces in the sink, and, at this time, there was no way I (or Snowy) could be blamed. This time I was hanging off the front door trying to obtain access to the property whilst Snowy was out on the town scavenging for her own survival. They now knew without question that Snowy and I were not the culprits for either incident.

A little bit of history - our Gloucester home, eight Gothic Cottages was a listed building having been built circa 1820 and used, along with the house next door, as an isolation house in the Cholera epidemic of 1832.

Craig and Parisa supposed between them that, in the nineteenth century, people had gone to the insolation house knowing that they were going to die which they had, eventually, accepted. They considered that some of those souls now remained there to share their energy with the here and now, which happened to be us lot at that time. After the wine glass shattering events they both regularly discussed the presence of other beings in the house, but always came to the same conclusion, that they were benevolent souls.

We were raised to keep an open mind

It was a good and kind supernatural feeling in that house. I could feel it. None of us were scared when our unseeable housemates occasionally made their presence known by the shutting of doors or moving of objects. It became part of the charm of the pretty little cottage in the heart of a busy city.

Whilst living at Hawkfield I had the privilege of being Lord Jenkins. My standing had not been challenged there as there were no other cats in the immediate vicinity. I, therefore, had a break from my previous past-time of cat fighting. However, in Gloucester City Centre there seemed to be an overpopulation of local cats who did not consider that I held any authority. Duelling, therefore, became a regular activity for me again in an effort to prove my worthiness.

Sitting in my palace without any power

These fights didn't always go in my favour. This was for two reasons. I was out of practice with my fighting skills having had a year-long sabbatical, and, I was now eleven years old so no longer a young cat. Most of the cats in the local neighbourhood were younger and stronger than me. I, sadly, regularly got defeated in my battles. My ears got ripped and I got various other war wounds, but this didn't deter me. I always licked my wounds clean and accepted and challenged new battles whenever they came about. I have always been persistent and determined and would remain so.

Armour up and say your prayers

My relationship with Stupid Lexi changed whilst living in Gloucester. One of the neighbours had a ginger tomcat. He and I did not agree on our view of the hierarchy of the cats in the local area and on a regular basis, we had LOUD and BIG discussions about this.

During one of these disagreements, Parisa heard from the house my fighting efforts and, in a moment of anxiety, opened the front door. Stupid Lexi immediately raced to my rescue and quickly placed her jaws firmly around the neck of my ginger ninja opponent. There was then a scream from Parisa whereupon the ginger tomcat was dropped and, sensibly, ran off.

I know that over the next few days, with no sign of the wimp, Parisa considered that Stupid Lexi may have fatally injured him, but, to her relief, he turned up, slightly weathered looking, a few days later. He never again came into our courtyard and I have Lexi to thank for that. She potentially saved my life and certainly re-established the boundary of our establishment and my hierarchy in the street. Perhaps she wasn't stupid after all? This was the second of my nine lives gone.

So, I'll be needing you

Snowy struggled with the transition of moving to Gloucester. She became even more withdrawn, only making appearances at meal times and then quickly disappearing again. She did well off the local takeaways too, but never shared her findings with me. I still shared with her though, when she was around, which became less and less.

One day she disappeared and, then, a couple of weeks later, the family had a phone call to say her microchip had been scanned at the local police station. She had, sadly, been hit by a car and died. Snowy had never been as streetwise or adaptable as me, and this ended up being her demise. I missed providing for and loving her.

Chapter 11

High hopes

We as a family spent just less than a year living in Gloucester. In June 2012 our house was to change again, but this one ended up being our long-term residence and the final place that I would call, 'Home'.

Go make a legacy

It was a bustling summer's day in the city of Gloucester and the busy atmosphere outdoors was mirrored on the inside of eight Gothic Cottages. Craig had hired a van and, for the third time in less than two years, all the Jenkins' family belongings were safely packed into it with the remnants jammed into the family estate car.

Parisa drove the BMW estate car whilst Craig was the designated driver of the removal van. Emily and Kayan now both 5 years old travelled with Craig in the van and Aaron (aged eight) Lexi, Steve (the family fire bellied toad), and I had the car as our mode of transport.

Always had high hopes

The short journeys I had previously encountered in motor vehicles had always been in the confines of a cat basket, but to my advantage, there was no room in the car for the basket so I had the comfort of Parisa's lap with the added luxury of freedom whilst travelling (a new concept and experience for me.)

I spent most of the journey curled up sleeping on Parisa's lap apart from a ten-minute interval about midway to our new destination where I exercised my new given freedom.

I always had a vision

I clambered into the boot of the car and proceeded to toilet. This was much to the disgust of Parisa and Aaron who could do absolutely nothing about it. When you have got to go, you've got to go – what else was I supposed to have done?

It's a little complicated

I enjoyed the motion of the car whilst travelling, it made me feel comfortable and rocked me to sleep. Poor Aaron had Steve's tank on his lap for the whole journey and any imperfections or bumps in the road were accompanied by a yelp from little Aaron as the water from the tank would, time and time again, splash over the top of the tank and onto him. Aaron got a substantial helping of frog water into his lap during the long journey which came to a crescendo on our arrival in Newquay due to a generous number of speed bumps that are scattered around the town's streets. When he came to leave his seat on arrival at our destination, it materialised that he was, literally, sitting in a puddle.

Despite Aaron's soggy bottom, the rather cramped conditions that everyone had travelled in for three and a half hours and the unpleasant smell that had accompanied my toilet moment, we all arrived safely in Trebarwith Crescent in Newquay quite late in the evening.

Steve, Lexi, and I were shut into the kitchen with food and water whilst the mass unloading of furniture and belongings was undertaken by the human members of the Jenkins' family. After the vehicles had been emptied of their contents it was bedtime, for everyone.

It had been a long tiring day of travelling and tomorrow would be my first day of exploration of my new home as, for that first night, I was contained with Lexi in the kitchen.

I was gonna be that one in a million

Chapter 12

King of my castle

The next day, the Jenkins' household was slow to rise. All the humans had slept on the floor in their new bedrooms. This was because most of our furniture had been left in Gloucester as the property was to be rented out to new tenants as furnished.

Lexi, Steve, and I had had the confines of the kitchen overnight, which, like the rest of the new home, presently had a very limited amount of furnishings other than towers of cardboard boxes.

The humans disappeared mid-morning (they had gone to buy beds for everyone) and the kitchen door was left ajar as a portal to the rest of the house. I took the opportunity, whilst everyone was out, to explore the substantial Victorian terrace.

Must be the reason why
I'm free in my threshold

The size of the property in comparison to Gothic Cottages was big, but it wasn't as huge as Hawkfield had been. It was a happy medium; large enough to not be on top of each other, but not so big in that one's voice wouldn't carry through the entire house – something that I would be sure to use to my advantage.

The high ceilings gave it a vast feeling; it felt very roomy. Large enough to swing a cat, but thankfully, that wasn't a past-time that any of the Jenkins' family partook in. The décor was dated, shabby, and tired– not cosy quaint and adhering like our previous home in Gloucester. It didn't have the same charm of the cottage. It felt very different but had an underlying feeling of potential. The original 1930s décor engulfed most of the house which included the original kitchen and a tatty old Aga cooker. Copious amounts of boxes of the cardboard variety overran the entire house. They were stacked high everywhere and looked like castle towers reaching upwards like stretched fingertips trying their best to touch the high ceilings.

I carefully examined each cardboard turret and, after much personal deliberation, selected the best and highest tower and proceeded with my determined ascent. It didn't take me long to reach the summit and, when I arrived at the top, I adopted my throne pose and admired my new kingdom.

Must be the reason why
I'm king of my castle

When the Jenkins' humans returned I was still sat at the top of my castle adopting my most regal position. All my minions admired and looked up to me. My status was clear. King Fudge had arrived and the town of Newquay better brace themselves as the REAL adventures were just about to begin.

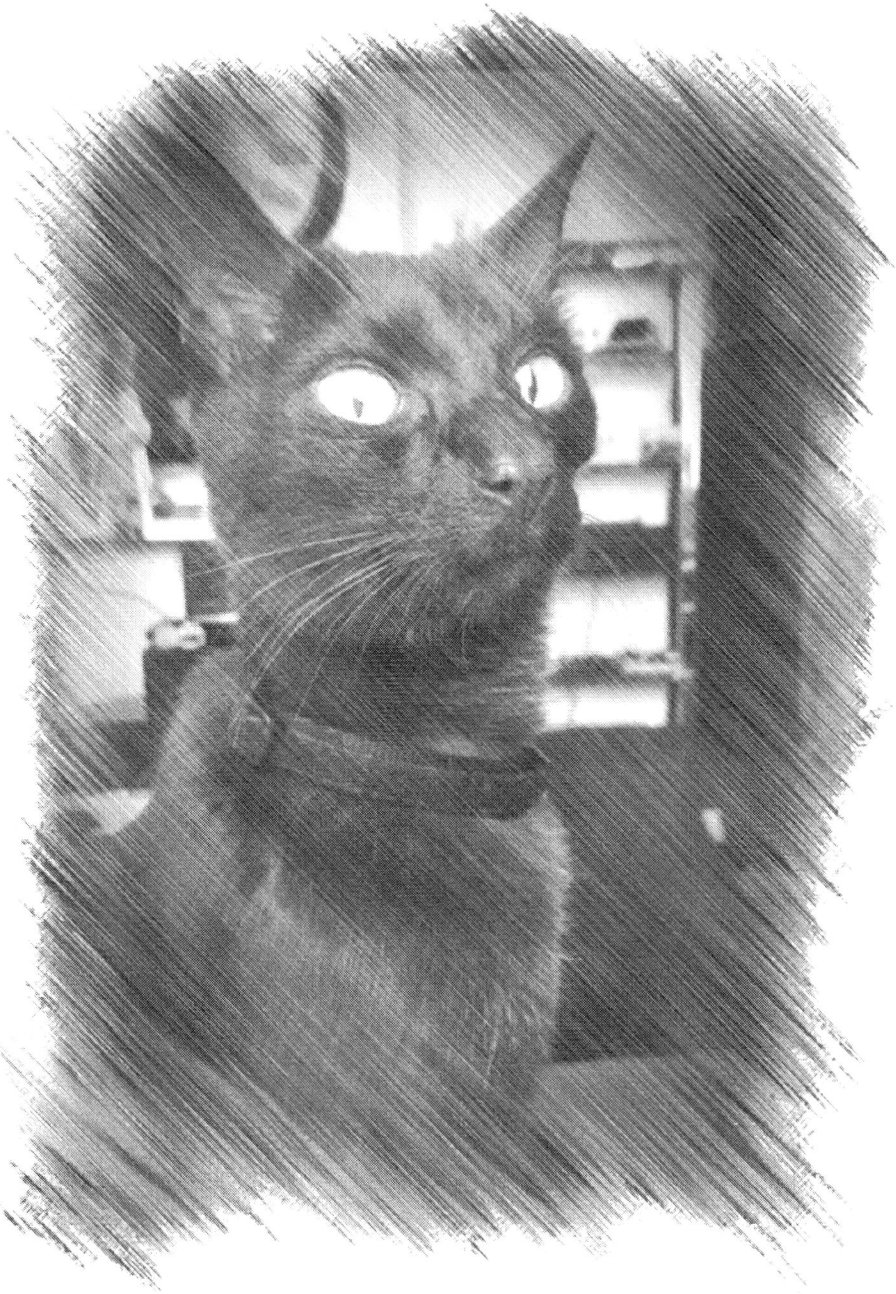

Chapter 13

Express yourself

Within a few days, I was allowed to venture outside and what a gem the town of Newquay was. It was heaven in my eyes. The convenience of a multitude of takeaways coupled with an unlimited amount of strangers who mostly appeared to be animal loving people.

I quickly set about taking full advantage of my new surroundings, including people who were open to persuasion when it came to sharing their food. There was lots of food around and it appeared that I did not have to put much effort in to obtain some of it. Although I could scavenge through the bins of the residents and the local restaurants, the most productive line of enquiry tended to be what I later learnt to be the 'tourists.'

Within 100 yards of the front door of our new home in Trebarwith Crescent was a green area called the Killacourt. This, in the summer months, was occupied for most of the day by happy souls who chose to frequent the area, many for the purpose of consuming food whilst appreciating the astounding views of Towan beach.

Very quickly I became very good at reading the tourists and ascertaining who was of generous nature and who was not. The result of this was that, on top of my two substantial and mandatory meals at home, I could easily obtain double the quantity of food if I spent a few hours hanging out on the Killacourt persuading people that I was underfed.

I took up this new role without question. I became a master of superb acting skills even if I do say so myself. I managed to increase the volume of my purring and would caress legs with my slender body which, most of the time, would result in them volunteering some food to me. After I had had my fill I would either sunbathe or head home depending on my mood.

Whatever you do, do it well

As a general rule, the front door would be shut on my arrival home, but I soon learnt how to open it. It was a PVC double glazed door and I found if I jumped and hung off the handle with all my body weight I could open it and let myself in. It only took me a few days to get my door opening skill to a really high-standard so that on the day of Craig and Parisa's wedding (just over two weeks after we had moved from Gloucester to Newquay) I helped Parisa's family know exactly which house was the Jenkins residence. I performed my catty acrobatic door opening skills with perfect timing in full view of the car full of visiting family as if providing an incredible cat butler service.

Being myself is something I do well

There were disadvantages as well as advantages of being able to go outside in a new area. The disadvantages were that, in the local established vicinity of cats, I was a stranger and, as had been the case in Gloucester, not always respected. I quickly made a few feline enemies.

A tuxedo cat- black with a white bib - became my main nemesis and we regularly loudly fought to try and ascertain who was top cat. He was considerably younger me which worked to his advantage. During most of our duels, I ended up being second place. Some of our battles would be brought to a premature end by interruption of a protective member of the Jenkins family who would hastily usher me back inside the house. This, apparently, was for my own good. I never agreed with this though, and so, would take up my argument with Tuxedo Nemesis cat as soon as feasibly possible.

Whatever I do, I do it good

There were two large *Alsatian* dogs that lived almost opposite our house on Trebarwith Crescent. Their human slave was a rather large bearded man who regularly chose to walk his dogs without the restraint of leads. This worked well for him and the dogs other than on the occasions where there were wandering cats in the street. Trebarwith Crescent had quite an impressive cat population so, more often than not, there would be wandering cats.

On these occasions, both dogs would take chase accompanied by Beardyman trying to convince them to give up their pursuit. His chosen method of persuasion would be shouting the dog's names at the top of his voice. I'm not sure whether the dogs heard him, or, chose not to hear him, but the constant conclusion I reached was that he was wasting his breath although the energy he exerted in his chosen method was commendable. I would have given him ten out of ten for effort.

Despite his lack of control of the dogs at these moments, thankfully, and to my knowledge, the cats always got away. Once the dogs had lost sight or the scent of the target cat they would finally return to Beardyman, who had been relentlessly calling them through the entire calamity. It was exciting, but frightening to watch.

One day whilst Tuxedo Nemesis and I were having one of our routine disagreements in the middle of the road, we were faced with Beardyman with his two dogs in tow. They were heading home from the supermarket I guess as plastic bags full of food were hanging from both Beardyman's arms. Needless to say, and to my disadvantage, neither of the dogs were on leads.

In what felt like a millisecond the dogs spotted both us cats and for reasons unknown to me they decided I was to be the cat target that day. They set about on their aggressive pursuit and Beardyman took up his usual activity of wasting his breath. I have never run so fast before in my life. I headed for the safety of our house. The dogs were on my heels immediately. I could feel their breath on my neck and the snarling and barking was overbearing. I ran down the middle of the street then darted between two parked cars to the front garden and clambered up the path. I launched myself at the door handle to attempt to open the door in what would have been a record-breaking acrobatic manoeuvre. Before I had even touched the handle and whilst in mid-air I felt jaws close around my body. I was then forcibly pinned to the front window of our house.

Trying to be a superstar like everybody else

Parisa was, fortunately, indoors and had heard the commotion. She came out of the front door with the energy of a lit cannon and leapt to my rescue by grabbing me from what I don't doubt were the jaws of death.

Lexi was in the house and Aaron had to hold her back as she, too, had heard the looming attack and was ready to protect me with her life; she was growling and barking like a creature possessed, but Parisa didn't need Lexi's back up. She had whipped me up and placed me back in the safety of the confines of the house shutting the front door whilst shooing off the dogs single-handedly.

She remained in the front garden until Beardyman had been able to retrieve his dogs and all his weekly shopping items which had been strewn all over the road during the terrifying ordeal.

I heard Parisa give Beardyman a mouthful about the lack of control he had over his animals, she vehemently said to him, 'Your dogs are going to end up killing my cat one day.' His confident reply was, 'Not if I can help it!'

Express yourself

Thankfully, after the events of that harrowing day, there was never to be another dog episode like that ever again in Trebarwith Crescent. I lost the third of my nine lives that day.

Chapter 14

Better together

My time in Newquay was about exploring - I always wanted to see more. As time went on I got braver and my inquisitive nature took me further afield than just the immediate vicinity of Trebarwith Crescent and the Killacourt.

My behaviour was more like that of a friendly dog. I loved spending time with people especially if there was a slither of a chance of getting food from them. Whilst outside I approached most people I met and would say, 'Hello,' in my loudest voice, if this got their attention I would then regularly use my tactic of rubbing my slender sleek body against their legs to encourage them to consider either, sharing food with me, or, giving me a fuss. If I felt people were open to sharing, but needed further encouragement I would reach my paw towards their food as if to point and make it perfectly clear what it was that I would like.

Sometimes I felt it necessary to follow people. This was for two reasons; the prospect of food and the opportunity to discover more of the big wild world with the added comfort and confidence of human company (my favourite type of company).

As the months passed I got to know the local area pretty well. There were lots of shops, eateries, people, and traffic (particularly in the summer months).

In June 2013 I decided to spend some time hanging out outside KFC on East Street. The smell there was so good. If only I could work out how to get hold of some of that finger lickin' chicken. I actually got somewhat mesmerised by the intoxicating smell, and, a little disorientated. I felt I just couldn't leave.

After three uninterrupted obsessive days of loitering outside, one of the employees took pity on me and carried me back to her home. She lived in a small bedsit with three other cats. They didn't really object to me joining the family and gave me the respect and personal space I demanded. Our lady carer was good to us all. She gave me loads of food and didn't mind where I toileted in her home, which was pretty much everywhere.

After four weeks I tired of the indoor environment and started to admire the outdoor space from the confines of the Victorian windowsill. One day whilst impatiently pacing the windowsill I spotted my family exiting the family car literally right outside. I put on my loudest voice and miraculously Aaron heard and saw me. Within thirty minutes I was back home as Parisa knocked on the door with such ferocity that I wouldn't be able to remain there for a second longer.

Unbelievably the property that I had been living in had been virtually opposite my home on Trebarwith Crescent and, following my stay with the lady carer and her three cats, I regularly revisited them. I was always welcome and given food and cuddles.

From the autumn of 2013 Parisa started spending less time at the house. I overheard a conversation that indicated she had acquired ownership of two horses, whatever they might be. She spent hours away from the house with them.

Yet another animal companion joined the Jenkins' clan in October 2013. Another dog. It seemed that Lexi needed a friend and Parisa wished to have company whilst visiting her horses who resided some six miles away from home.

Bella was the name of the new canine companion and there was only one way to describe her; she was absolutely mental. I've never known an animal with so much energy and so little intelligence. She bounced up and down like a kangaroo squealing and barking with excitement and being anywhere near her made me feel utterly exhausted. She had just too much enthusiasm and so every time she bounced near to me I would growl loudly and back it up with a swipe at her nose with my paw if my mood required it.

Her main objective seemed to constantly be to waste energy by being far too physically active for no particular reason. She got excited when it was time for her and Lexi to go for a walk (I would have to investigate for myself whether these 'walks' were exciting). She got excited when someone knocked on the door (not exciting). She got excited when it was food time (arguably exciting.) She got excited when people started talking to her (not exciting). She pretty much got excited about everything - most of which were not exciting activities. Her breed was Patterdale crossed with Springer Spaniel and she was to regularly accompany Parisa to the horses - that was her main job. I was always pleased to see her leave with Parisa in the mornings, 'Go burn some energy off you lunatic!' is what I used to sing to her loudly as she tugged Parisa out of the front door with the power and force of a steam train.

Lexi seemed to love her though and so did Parisa. I considered despite her frantic persona and the fact that she irritated me with her lack of intelligence and over enthusiasm for everything, she made members of my family happy, so she did actually belong with us. She served a purpose for beings other than myself. Happiness is something everyone deserves and Bella seemed to have mountains of it to share.

Love is the answer

A few weeks passed and Bella's enthusiasm for everything didn't lessen. My initial objection to her and her annoying over excitability did waver a bit and I started to ponder whether the excitable behaviour prior to the walks that she and Lexi got taken on in the morning might be justified. I decided it needed personal investigation and stalked Craig, Parisa, Bella, and Lexi as they left the house one morning before breakfast. They pottered to the Killacourt and then headed down the concrete steps onto a small boulevard (where the Sea Life Centre building resides) then down further concrete steps onto Towan beach. I followed them.

When the morning light sings and brings new things

This new environment was interesting. There were waves, sand, pebbles, people, and other dogs. I didn't see any other cats though. When unknown dogs approached me, Parisa became concerned. She would lift me up before they got close and she would not put me down again until the dogs had either lost interest in me or been called off by their owner. She needn't have worried really as I was now quite capable of telling any dumb dog to go away with my loud growls and my piercing right hook. Her worry did, however, reiterate how much she cared for me. It was protective love.

Whilst we were all on the beach Lexi and Bella would run and run and run until they could run no more. There seemed no logic, no specific direction and no final destination in mind. It was chaotic and frenetic. On occasion, either Parisa or Craig would throw a stone for them to chase. As neither of them were blessed with large brains it didn't matter who the stone was thrown for, both of them would pursue it and, nine times out of ten, Bella being the younger and fitter of the two, would collect it. Lexi would then spend quite a lot of time chasing Bella in the hope that she might tire of the toy. Neither of them appreciated that the beach had an over population of stones which surrounded them and they could choose any they wanted to play with at any moment without having to chase those that had been selected by our humans.

I accompanied them on all of these walks for the next few days and made general observations. The walks would always start on the

Killacourt and, if the tide was out, it would often then involve some time on the beach.

Our dreams and they are made out of real things

A constant theme of these walks was toileting. Craig and Parisa encouraged both dogs to toilet before they went down to the beach. Interesting. I decided I should join in with this family activity and would spray the bushes and then wander to the garden of the nearby retirement home that fronts the Killacourt where I selected an impressive flowerbed in which to make my deposit. This didn't impress the owner of said flowerbed and Parisa and Craig did apologise to the resident for my choice of toilet location.

Too many things I have to do

I think Bella was perhaps a little over the top in her mandatory pre-walk dance and song that she did every morning, but there were worse ways to start the day. The main advantage for me to these morning walks was that all the while I could sing my 'I'm hungry' song loudly until we returned home so that absolutely everybody was aware that I needed breakfast.

From that day on I decided that morning walks with the family was something that I would regularly incorporate into my daily routine. A refreshing walk with friends before breakfast was actually very nice.

Jenkins family bliss ensued and for about nine months all was quiet and happy and simple. We had all adapted to our new home of Newquay and we're making friends and memories; happy times.

Yeah, it's always better when we're together

In July 2014 that all changed. Something awful happened. The happy family unit broke and the question that brought about this chaos was, 'Where's Bella?'

Chapter 15

Walking with elephants

On the evening of 13 July 2014, the backdoor of the Jenkins' home was carelessly left open with devastating consequences. Mental Bella disappeared without a trace.

Parisa lost herself in guilt and worry and detached herself from the family. She went totally inward and didn't interact with anyone much. She didn't hear or notice my calls for food and drink and attention, and, believe me, I made lots of them.

For the next two months, she searched for Bella every single day. She exhausted herself mentally and physically looking for that stupid dog. It was her only focus. She withdrew herself from family interaction and I heard Craig say she was on the verge of a mental breakdown, which I think was a fair observation. She was certainly very unhappy and very stressed and would not take comfort from anyone, not even me. She just brushed me away when I tried to comfort her.

Parisa launched a huge search online and in person with over 2,000 people trying to help FindBella. Thankfully, Bella was found eight weeks later on 11 September 2014 over 200 miles away in Kidderminster having been stolen by a holidaymaker - but that's another story.

Bella came home to us shortly after and Parisa returned in mind and spirit to her previous self. The family unit was back to usual happiness with everyone being attended to as they should be. I, for one, was glad to see Bella back. Not because I had missed her nutty behaviour, but, more because of how ecstatic Lexi and Parisa were to see her.

Almost immediately, Bella's over enthusiasm brought joy to the house again. Poor Lexi had grieved dreadfully for Bella the entire time she had been missing. Her eyes had mirrored those of Parisa's, low, sullen, and empty, but, now, again, they were bright, full of life and sparkle; everyone was smiling again. It was back to our normal family household and my calls for food and water were adhered to once more.

Shortly after Bella's return, we attained two new members of the Jenkins family of the feline variety in the form of tiny pure Siamese kittens, one chocolate, one seal point; both males.

Yet again the family focus wandered off me. I wasn't happy about this and I didn't particularly like either of them much. They were full of mischief, energy, enthusiasm, and curiosity. I took to hissing at them with maximum effort whenever they came close to me.

Although this was an effective way of getting my point across their curiosity and what seemed like goldfish like memory would mean that no sooner had I sent them running with a menacing hiss they would return for a second attempt to say, 'Hello.' I wasn't having any of it though and would repeat my hiss slightly louder than last time.

It was exhausting and annoying to continually tell them to go away. I got regularly told by our humans that my behaviour towards the babies was not nice or necessary. I agree that it may not have been nice but, as far as I was concerned, it was necessary. Their presence upset me and I have always been an open book when it comes to feelings, I'm not one to pretend everything is alright when it's not.

Phoenix was the chocolate baby. There was a physical resemblance between him and I as kittens although he had very large ears and I wondered if he would ever grow into them. His personality was kind, soft, affectionate, and loving but not brave or independent. He thrived on company.

Orlando was the seal point baby. He reminded me of Snowy. He had the same mesmerising blue eyes that would take your breath away and an independent but somewhat selfish personality.

They were playful and energetic and had shrill loud voices, particularly at meal times. The humans were infatuated with these two new members and covered them in kisses and cuddles in what I would describe an obsessive way. My needs were pushed aside a little whilst the kittens settled in. This was unacceptable by my standards.

My unhappy hissing continued for some weeks, I put a lot of effort into the dramatisation of my discontent. A month later, I started to feel unwell. I'm not sure whether my dramatic unhappy efforts caused my illness but they probably didn't help. I went from feeling a bit unwell one morning to, within three days, being really, really ill.

It was about time the focus of all the family members swung to solely sit with me and that is exactly what happened.

Chapter 16

Magic

It was mid-October 2014 when I fell ill. My tummy hurt, going to the toilet was uncomfortable, and I found eating and drinking something I really didn't fancy doing.

I just got broken

After three days Parisa took me to the vets as she was concerned about my welfare. I was poked and prodded then sent home with some probiotic paste which was to be given to me three times a day for five days along with water – both were to be syringed into my mouth. When Parisa tried to follow the vet's instructions, I objected. I really objected. There was lots of hissing, growling and scratching. The water and the paste were things I did not want at all.

My protests against the medication and administration of water were futile, I realised this by the end of the first day and so set about a more effective line of protest. I used my voice at maximum volume to sing my song, 'Let me out of here NOW.' It was my musical request to be let outside that I thought would eventually work. It paid off.

After singing all through the night my request was adhered to and the front door was opened to let me venture out. I set off to my usual hangout of the Killacourt and lay down. I was relieved to be outside where no more paste or water would be forced upon me. My freedom was short-lived though as a stranger took pity on me and took me to the vets where I was scanned. The call was made to Craig for him and Parisa to pick me up which they did promptly.

When I returned home it was paste and water time again which, of course I objected to. I decided to adopt the same method as last time and began my song mid-afternoon with even more volume than last time.

In the early hours of the following morning, the front door was opened by Parisa to enable me to go out again as the whole household had had enough of my constant loud and tiresome song. This time I had a whole day of relaxing and not being bothered by anyone. I spent time lying in the flowerbeds of the retirement home resting and generally feeling poorly but, at least I wasn't being forced to have that disgusting paste and water. Yet again someone took pity on me. This time the person looked official and I read the letters RSPCA on the vehicle that I was placed into. I was taken back to the vets, again.

I was poked and prodded again; this time with various needles (some blood was taken) and then placed back in an enclosure alongside other small unwell animals.

After what seemed like a long-time I was taken into a consulting room where a nurse and a vet stood over me looking solemn. The door to the room swung open with force and in came Parisa. Her eyes were wide and there was a strong feeling of determination coming from her. She was a force to be reckoned with.

I felt really unwell and tired so wasn't really sure what was happening or what the topic of conversation was at the time but I could just about follow the scene that unfolded in front of me.

Parisa said, firmly, 'I would like to know what the options are and then I will make an educated decision.'

The vet looked quite shocked by the question but, after a short pause replied, 'There are no options, he will not recover.'

Parisa was clearly not satisfied with his reply so she then said, 'OK, if Fudge was human what could be done to try and help him?'

The vet's reply was immediate and confident, 'There would be nothing we could do, he would suffer a little longer then die. The kindest thing would be to put him to sleep now.'

Parisa then sternly said, 'I would not be able to live with myself if I didn't try to help our long-standing family friend of 15 years. He has not yet had any full course of medication, only a probiotic paste. I am simply not prepared to give up on him just yet. If you will not try and help him I will find someone who is prepared to give him a chance. Please tell me that there is something that you can at least try?'

The vet looked taken aback. There was, for a few long seconds, an uncomfortable silence. He then said, tentatively, 'Well, we could try putting him on a drip but I don't think….'

He didn't get a chance to finish his sentence before Parisa curtly cut him off, 'YES, let's do that!'

I was taken out of the consultation room. A needle was put into my right leg where it stayed pumping fluid into me and then I was carefully placed back in the enclosure where, for two days, I stayed and rested. I, slowly, started to feel a little stronger and better. At the end of those two days I felt like eating a little and Parisa came to the vets and, with tears of relief, took me home.

I later heard she had put out a plea on Facebook for people to send positive thoughts to me to try and help me heal. I believe it did help me in my recovery.

For the following two weeks, Parisa hardly let me out of her sight and I spent hours and hours with her, mostly curled up on her lap. She poured love into me. I could feel it emanating from her hands as they rested gently on me.

She hand-fed me all different types of food (chicken, prawns, fish, steak) three times a day and offered me fresh water drinks from the tap every now and then when she thought I might be thirsty. I got to travel in the car with her, curled up on her lap whilst she drove and, for the first time in my life got to meet the horses as she took me with her to them every day.

Whilst she set about feeding and tending to her horses I sat patiently on the driver's seat watching her intently through the window. If I lost sight of her I would call out for her and she would come running to the car and reassure me that she was still there and nearly finished. She took me for walks outside of the house on a lead. It was my first experience of walking on a lead and I found it an absolute breeze. I actually hardly noticed that there was a lead attached to my collar. It was more like escorted walks as she just followed me slowly wherever I wanted to go. I mainly sauntered to the Killacourt or the alleyway at the back of the house where I would toilet if I so wished and then roll around on my back in the dust.

I don't want anyone else but you

A fortnight later I was feeling much more normal and I was eating and drinking without assistance. Parisa gently picked me up and said we were going off for a car journey together. I assumed we were off to the horses again but no, on this occasion we went to a new vet where I was examined. I heard the vet say that I was in good health apart from a little underweight which I knew Parisa was relieved to hear.

It seems I had cheated death again and I clearly have Parisa to thank for her assistance. This was my fourth life down.

Call it magic

I felt quite smug that I had managed to completely change the attitude of this woman towards me. She had gone from dictating when I could eat and ignoring my requests for fresh water drinks straight from the tap to abiding to my every request. She now shared all her meals with me, feed me on demand, provided fresh water drinks for me straight from the tap whenever I wanted them and took me for walks on the lead wherever I wanted to go. I was pleased with my persuasion work.

Parisa really was becoming my most favourite and attentive human slave and I felt lucky to have her in my life and by my side. For several weeks, as a thank you for her help nursing me back to health, I took to sleeping curled up by her head every night when she went to bed.

Chapter 17

Nothings gonna stop us now

As the weeks passed I put my weight back on and returned to 100 per cent health. Once Parisa was satisfied that I was fully recovered I got my freedom back and was allowed to venture outside the house again by myself. It was time to get back to business.

The world that I've found is too good to be true

My objectives were to eat copious amounts of food, get to know as many people as possible and explore as far as possible.

As Phoenix and Orlando were house cats and, unlike me, were not afforded the freedom and luxury of outdoor time, I decided that they needed to experience street food and that I should be their provider. I had enjoyed providing for Snowy all those years ago and this wasn't much different. Once I had had my fill of food that I gathered from various outdoor sources, I would take home remnants for the two kittens.

On reaching the front door, I would adopt my old song, 'I have food.' After varying lengths of howling time (depending who was at home and their location in the house) the front door would be opened and I would step in and drop the food on the porch floor for Phoenix and Orlando to eat. I always enjoyed being a hunter/gatherer and my return to this role was reminiscent and became regular. I liked providing for others.

Just because I brought food parcels home for the babies didn't mean I liked them. I wouldn't say I liked them - I tolerated them. I brought them street food purely because I like to provide for others, that's it.

Both Phoenix and Orlando grew into beautiful elegant cats. From time to time they would invade my personal space when I was not in the mood. I dealt with this by way of a growl and a bop on the head. This always saw Orlando off as he was not brave, Phoenix would however sometimes stand up to me and I would have to increase my volume and physical effort to get him to leave me alone. He was a bit feisty and reminded me of myself.

I had learnt over the years that in order to have food shared with me at the Jenkins mealtimes a polite and patient attitude was essential. Phoenix and Orlando didn't get this at all.

Come meal times they would attempt to lift food off the plates with either their mouths or outstretched paws which would result in a gentle smack on the nose and them being locked out of the kitchen whilst the family meal was consumed.

Without fail my method resulted in my staying sat at the dinner table and being hand-fed delicious morsels. One day those two cretins would work out that my method worked but for now Orlando and Phoenix would be excluded from family meal times because of their stupidity.

Before I had become ill there had been considerable building work going on at the end of Trebarwith Crescent on the site that used to be Newquay bus station. By the time I had recovered from my illness and got back my freedom and independence, the building work had been completed and two restaurants had moved into two of the units.

I started to familiarise myself with the set-up of both restaurants and made friends with many of the staff. One was an Italian pasta and pizza restaurant and the other an American diner.

I found if I loitered outside the American diner it was mainly a fortuitous experience. The manager of this diner was a guy named James and he was very warm towards me although, most times he found me lurking either inside or outside the restaurant performing my song 'I'm starving,' he would pick me up and march me back home.

Put your hand in my hand, baby. Don't ever look back

The manager of the other restaurant was not so kindly. He didn't appreciate my persistent company inside or outside his restaurant and in what can only be described as an unfriendly manner would chase me off and make it very clear to staff and customers that I was not welcome there at all.

On one occasion Parisa got wind of his harsh manner. In an abrupt way one evening she visited the restaurant and told said manager if she ever heard that he had stamped on me again she would be reporting his actions to the police.

I didn't frequent that restaurant again after that occasion, he wasn't kind, he wasn't an animal loving person and I didn't want to interact with him again. It actually suited me not going there again, I didn't really like Italian food anyway. I think it's overrated.

Let the world around us just fall apart

I still persisted next door at the American diner though as the staff there seemed to appreciate and love me. The food was also pretty good.

In the summer of 2015 access to food at this venue became even easier. In hot weather, the door would be left open enabling me to wander in and make myself comfortable. Guests also had the option of dining outside on sunny days and I found that some could be persuaded to share their food with me.

One of my favourite pastimes was immersing myself in outdoor bins. The bin outside one of the neighbouring houses that I liked to frequent and the bins on the Killacourt were my favourites. They were particularly deep and could hold some tremendous pickings that were usually buried quite far down. My technique of acquiring food from them was intense and required focus and concentration.

I found if I balanced on the opening and then proceeded to dig downwards in a rabbit like manner I could eventually immerse all of my body (except my tail) inside the bin and access the dark depths which would more than likely contain some delicious treats such as chicken bones or fish and chip wrappers.

My excavations would sometimes be interrupted by one of the Jenkins' spoil sports if they spotted my tail poking out of bins. I would be plummeted back into the light as they rudely extracted me from my treasure hunting.

During my daily wanderings I would regularly bump into a nice gentleman called Riko. He liked to wear a red tee shirt and shorts (irrespective of the weather) and post letters and parcels through people's letterboxes. I didn't judge him for his strange hobby. It's quite common to have unusual pastimes; each to their own is what I say.

Let 'em say we're crazy
I don't care about that

He was a friendly guy and would always chat with me. He would stroke me in a way that made me know that he really appreciated my beauty and personality. I enjoyed seeing him and spending a few minutes in his company.

The local taxi rank at the end of Trebarwith Crescent, which overlooks the Killacourt, was also one of my hangouts. Two of the taxi drivers, Jo and Steve were particularly kind. They knew me by name and I came to understand they were friends of Parisa and Craig.

I liked visiting the Killacourt. I started accompanying Lexi and Bella on their morning walks again but also got back to visiting there at other times of the day by myself. It was a popular place for dog walking for many people. This proved to be, mainly, a source of annoyance for me.

I liked to patrol the area at a leisurely pace and did not appreciate being harassed by inquisitive, dumb dogs. Quite frequently I had to loudly remind various mutts to not come too close to me. If my loud growl didn't get the point across then a swipe at the nose would generally suffice.

Thankfully none of the dogs I came across were aggressive like the Alsatians that lived opposite and, obviously, the advantage of them being walked on the Killacourt was that most people had them contained on leads which meant if they weren't overly friendly to me, and didn't take my unsubtle hints, their owners would pull them away.

Standing strong forever

There were various cafes on East Street that pumped out the incredible smell of good cooked food, With the company of a feline accomplice (one of the local young cats that I took under my wing) I spent some time hanging out around the back of Bunters café where the staff would provide us with small amounts of hot food from time to time.

The fish and chip shops in the town were a good source of food for me too. Not directly of course, but many people, particularly in the summer months were partial to fish and chips and would like to enjoy eating it either on the beach or the Killacourt. I would offer my company to them and smile and chat to them with different levels of success.

There were lots of shops all through Newquay centre and, as time went on, I felt it necessary to visit most of them. Coffee shops, charity shops, art galleries, sandwich shops – I went to them all and it resulted in me being well known and, generally, liked.

My friendly and inquisitive nature resulted in getting myself into various situations in which it seemed I needed assistance to return home.

Whatever it takes
I will stay here with you

One day I took a fancy to a couple who were walking through the Killacourt and decided to follow them. We ended up at Newquay harbour; a fascinating area that I hadn't visited before. There is a shallow beach there with a restaurant fronting it and the enclosed harbour area houses a collection of small boats (mostly of the fishing variety). These quaint boats sit patiently on the surface of the sea quietly waiting for their next adventure to begin.

The air there is filled with the amazing aroma of fresh fish. I spent some time inhaling deeply trying to ascertain the source that generated such a wondrous smell. However, my investigation was cut short by my new human friends who considered I must be lost and took me to a vet's on the outskirts of the town. My microchip was scanned there and Craig and Parisa received a phone call asking them to come and collect me. This was my fifth live down.

Parisa was a bit annoyed when she came to pick me up, she muttered that I was a bit of a pest but I knew she didn't really mean it. She, like everyone, adored me.

I'm so glad I found you,
I'm not gonna lose you

I rode shotgun in the car for the two-mile journey home from the vets with my front paws firmly on the dashboard the whole way so I could get a clear view out of the windscreen. It was mesmerising watching everything move so fast. I very much enjoyed car journeys.

On returning home, I was kept inside the house for a couple of days but, after I increased the volume of my vocal demands for outside experience, I was allowed out again and resumed my mission.

A few weeks later I was busy patrolling East Street checking out the various eateries and shops when I decided I should return home, perhaps via my favourite restaurant Frankie and Benny's, as I was feeling a little hungry.

I went to cross the road when I heard a soft but concerned voice say, 'Don't cross just yet.' I turned around to see a lady with a gentle face accompanied by her three children stood not far from the ice-cream parlour. She smiled at me confirming she had been the giver of the advice. Maybe she had some food for me? I was keen to try ice-cream having seen so many skilfully snatched by seagulls from unsuspecting hands. I definitely wanted to see if it tasted nice – maybe this was my chance?

I ran over to the family to investigate. Quite brilliantly they knew my name! I asked loudly several times if they had any food for me but they didn't answer and didn't offer me any which was disappointing. I then adopted my stalker persona in the hope that following them would result in some eventual offerings of food. We all strolled quite a long way up East Street together.

Take you to the good times, see you through the bad times

After a reasonable pursuit, the lady lovingly picked me up and carried me back home. She placed me outside my home on Trebarwith Crescent and then went to leave. I didn't want her to go so I followed – still hopeful of some sort of food offerings. She scooped me up several times and put me back outside my home and time and time again I followed. Eventually, she picked me up and just cradled me like a baby – I enjoyed that and lapped up the affection. Ten minutes later Parisa turned up.

'Thank you, Louise,' she said as Louise passed me over. Parisa took me inside the house and gave me some food.

My plan had worked in a roundabout sort of way and potentially on that day Louise had saved my life by calling my name. Sixth life down.

In October 2015 I went on a longer car journey than the usual short trips that had become the norm since we moved to Newquay. I travelled from Newquay to Perranporth (some ten miles) with the Jenkins family. Together we ventured from the car park, across the beach to The Watering Hole pub and restaurant where I shared fish and chips with Parisa. It was a lovely trip out with the family but as far as car journeys went, it wasn't a patch on the journey I would make by myself a year later.

Nothing's gonna stop us, nothing's gonna stop us now

Chapter 18

Lovely day

The year 2016 was a busy year for me.

When I wake up in the morning, love

Most mornings, after my breakfast (which included at least two fresh water drinks from the sink), would involve a walk on the beach with friends. After walking the dogs and helping various children family members finish their breakfast I would try my luck at getting a car ride to the stables. When Parisa left the house to take the children to school, I followed. I knew the routine they would go to the garage, retrieve the car, and then Parisa would take the children to school before heading on to the horses.

I scurried behind them and there tended to be lots of muttering at me to get out of the way as Parisa tried to reverse out of the garage without flattening me. Quite often I would be bundled into the car so that she could reverse out confident that I wouldn't be in her path. Whether or not I got to stay for the journey was unpredictable. Sometimes I would be allowed to stay, and, other times, once the garage had been shut, I would be carefully placed outside before they drove away. I was always disappointed when I didn't get to go with them.

On the occasions I did get to stay with them I would sit with the kids in the back of the car until they got dropped at school when I would then relocate to the front and curl up on Parisa's lap. Some days we would then go to the petrol station where Parisa would refuel. The staff at Gannel Road garage got used to seeing me perched in the passenger seat and they would ask after me now and then, which I thought was caring of them.

After filling up Parisa would sometimes frequent McDonald's where she would buy me a Sausage McMuffin. I would sit patiently in the passenger seat whilst we waited at the drive thru window for our food to be prepared, both of us trying not to salivate with anticipation.

Next stop would be the horses and I would either patrol the perimeter of the fields, sunbathe on the bonnet or snooze or sit in the car whilst Parisa attended to her business. Whatever I chose to do it always felt productive.

The times that I didn't go with Parisa to the horses I would busy myself at home and in the streets of Newquay. Anytime I spent at home was split between three activities; eating, sleeping, and toileting.

And the world's alright with me

I ate at least twice a day at home; breakfast and supper. If I hung around the kitchen at lunch and/or dinner time I could generally convince Craig and Parisa to share their food. I became accustomed to on average four meals a day. I also of course acquired food outside of the house at various different locations.

I slept on the sofa, the booth in the kitchen, or one of the many beds in the house whenever I felt tired. Because I started regularly demanding in the early hours of the morning for outside time and was constantly using most areas in the house (except the litter tray) as my personal toilet, it was decided that I should spend the nights outside.

A cat bed was placed at the front door for my convenience and I would spend some of the night leisurely sauntering then would put myself to bed in said cat bed when I needed to sleep. I slept well there. It was comfortable and clean and actually just the right temperature.

When sleeping indoors I almost always had to endure the heat of Phoenix and Orlando as quite often they would decide that the sleeping area I had chosen was to be a 'cat family' experience. I was generally in two minds about whether this annoyed me or not. Sometimes it would annoy me and I would growl and relocate, and, other times, I tolerated it because it wasn't too bad.

The night time routine was well established I would be placed outside the front door when the family went to bed and the call of Newquay nightlife summoned me. One evening when I was dreaming of chasing rabbits I was woken quite abruptly from my comfortable slumber on Parisa and Craig's bed. A heated discussion followed between them both where the topic of argument was, 'who should be the one to take me downstairs?'

An agreement was reached and rather than escort me down the two flights of stairs and put me outside the front door (as was the routine) I was placed outside the skylight which happens to be on the third floor. I slowly but reasonably gracefully skied down the metre and half slope and landed squarely on the flat roof of Kayan's bedroom.

I was quite put out by this rough wakeup call and break of routine and quickly noticed that there was no easy route for me to take to get down to ground level. It was roughly a two metre drop down which, at my mature age, was something I was not prepared to attempt.

To voice my distress and disgust at being put in such a predicament I started to yowl for help, very loudly. The more time that passed without help, the louder my song became (my lung capacity is outstanding).

I vaguely heard a further heated discussion between Parisa and Craig. Several lights from many bedrooms in the surrounding properties were now coming to life. At least I was getting everyone's attention.

For some unknown reason, Parisa and Craig thought it the time to dangle bedding out of the skylight at me. Did they think this was a time to play? Were they deluded?

I started to pace the edge of the roof looking carefully for any possible escape route to the safety of the ground. After several circuits, I heard a voice. It was Craig peering at me with only his eyes visible above the flat roof height.

He looked unbalanced and I considered he must be standing on something that compromised his sense of gravity. He also looked a bit cross – like he does when I haven't used the litter tray. I decided that being near him at this time was not a good idea.

Just one look at you and I know it's gonna be

Craig had other ideas clearly, and, before I had a chance to extend the distance between us both, he had managed to wrap his hand firmly around my middle.

What flashed through my mind at this point was the immense drop to ground level and I considered my journey down from the roof would likely include an uncomfortable or unforgiving landing particularly as I could now see that Craig was precariously balancing on a narrow windowsill in the unusual attire of just his underwear. In a last-minute moment of self-preservation, I grabbed at the telephone lines with my claws and managed to capture them.

I let out my combined celebration and objection screech as Craig wrestled me from the comfort of the telephone lines whilst calling me several unflattering names. Victorious and furious Craig climbed back through Kayan's bedroom window with me tucked safely under this arm accompanied by cheering and clapping from the neighbours who had been silently watching our double act show from the shadows of their balcony.

I was walked downstairs to a gentle but loving scolding whilst all the while in the background I could hear laughter.

A lovely day

'Goodnight Fudge,' said Craig, as he put me outside the front door where I contemplated my next episode.

Chapter 19

Everywhere

I enjoyed the freedom that being put out at night gave me. The town centre was actually a very different place at night than in the day. The clientele was different too; you didn't get many young families around eating on the Killacourt. It seemed to be more of a hangout for drinking and loud socialising than eating and enjoying the view. It always was interesting to watch, from a distance.

I found many of the night people to be less friendly towards me so I tended to keep my distance from and lurk in the shadows. Streetwise was my middle name.

Come the morning I would generally wake before any of the Jenkins' clan having slept in my comfortable cat bed in the front garden. My belly would be empty and, in order to spur my human slaves into action, I would promptly begin my first daily mission of access house and get food. Whilst catapulting myself at the front door handle with all my strength in an effort to reach the handle and open the door, I would embark on my loudest and most demanding catty song - a combination of two of my favourites, 'Let me in now' and 'I'm starving.' This personal concert of magnificent volume would result in the door being opened and me being hastily ushered in and fed. I am convinced that my efforts always meant the door was opened sooner than would have been the case if I hadn't embarked on my acrobatic and vocal mission.

Can you hear me calling?

Newquay is a popular place for surfing and Craig had thrown himself into the sea for the purpose of partaking in this hobby when we moved to Newquay. Surfing, from what I could see, involved putting on a skin-tight neoprene one-piece suit (which I have to admit wasn't the most flattering) and then spending several hours trying to balance on what looked like an ironing board (without legs) in the turbulent sea. It was a strange thing to do but you know what my view is on unusual past times.

Craig had several surfing buddies who, too, enjoyed the balancing task whilst negotiating waves. One of these friends was called Jake and he came to the house quite often where he and Craig would suit up and go and spend a few hours in the sea together taking it in turns to fall-off their boards.

I didn't really like Jake, he often came to the house consuming a Subway sandwich (Subway is by far my favourite sandwich provider) and he would not, despite my loud and unsubtle hints, ever share any of it with me. I considered this mean of him and looked for an opportunity to make my dissatisfaction known to him. An idea came to me pretty quickly.

Everything in the house at Trebarwith Crescent belonged to me. This was common knowledge; our home was my kingdom and I would regularly mark my territory.

One day Jake came to the house with the intention of surfing later on with Craig. There was a conversation between him and Craig about lunch and they left the house with the intention of feeding themselves.

Jake left his wetsuit in a box on the kitchen floor. As soon as I heard the front door shut without delay I set about putting my idea into action. I scurried over to the box that housed Jake's wetsuit and proceeded to urinate in it. It was satisfying.

When I heard the boys returning home after lunch, I ran upstairs and hid under Aaron's bed as I knew neither of them would be pleased with my toileting. They immediately discovered said marking of territory and, despite Craig's mammoth effort of rinsing the wetsuit several times through in the shower, Jake had to go surfing accompanied with 'odour de cat urine' courtesy of Fudge Jenkins. From then on whenever Jake came to the house with his wetsuit he would make sure that it was placed in a cupboard to avoid me marking it again. He never did share his sandwiches with me though.

Whilst innocently wandering on Towan Beach by the Sea Life centre on a sunny June morning, another well-meaning tourist wrongly considered I was lost and transported me to the vets where I was scanned resulting in Parisa and Craig coming to collect me.

This kind of incident was becoming quite a regular occurrence and Parisa was getting a little fed up of it. She decided to buy me a tag that I then wore on my collar. It had my name on one side and Craig's mobile phone number on the other.

Something's happening, happening to me

I was spending considerable amounts of time on the streets of Newquay in the summer months for the purpose of scavenging food and general exploration. I would regularly spend time at Frankie and Benny's (the American Diner at the end of the road), Subway, the fish and chip shop, the various café's, the appropriately named Fudge shop, the Cancer Research Charity shop and some other local shops.

Many people that I bumped into on my travels around Newquay chose to call the phone number on my tag to check that I wasn't lost. Craig's standard reply, once they advised him of my location, was, 'No, he's not lost.'

Most of the time I was on the Killacourt or at one of the eateries or shops on East Street. Shortly after such a phone call Craig, Parisa, or one of the kids would come and retrieve me and take me home.

East Street was a busy road; it was a thoroughfare for all sorts of traffic; pedestrians, cyclists, skateboarders, taxi's, cars, buses, coaches, and motorbikes.

In the summer, the traffic up that road would be heavy. It really didn't bother me how much traffic was on the road. I had two gears that I travelled at; expectant when there was the prospect of food, and nonchalant (unless I was being pursued by Alsatians).

On one afternoon in August, the busiest month of the year in Newquay, I was sauntering along the middle of East Street without a care in the world. I could hear shouting and loud long beeping filling the street which appeared to be coming from behind me. I couldn't really be bothered to look around and see the source of the commotion as it really didn't interest me.

I carried on walking slowly in the middle of the road until I reached the turning to Trebarwith Crescent where I paused. Whilst I considered my next move there was another loud long beep behind me, which, I, again, ignored. I finally decided I would call into Frankie and Benny's and see my friends and maybe eat some food.

As I turned down Trebarwith Crescent leaving East Street behind, a double decker bus, which had obviously been virtually stationary behind me the whole time I had walked up the hill, continued its journey up East Street over-revving. The driver shouted something inaudible at me and shook his fist. What was his problem?

My friends say I'm acting peculiarly

When it came to scavenging food on the streets, my main competition was the seagulls. I watched them closely; they were experts, even by my standards. Their methods of obtaining food were enviable but, in my opinion, a little aggressive. I preferred to negotiate with my potential contributors of food. The seagulls just saw their opportunities and went in for the snatch.

Their success rate was higher than mine but I like to think I was better liked then them. I was humbler and subtler in my approach, and, if people really didn't want to share with me I accepted that.

Seagulls did not care if people didn't want to share their food; if they considered that they could obtain food from specific people (mainly unsuspecting tourists) they would take it, without asking or caring about the answer.

They didn't come across as particularly intelligent birds either. Whenever one of them did manage to steal some food, rather than quickly and quietly enjoy consuming it, they would announce to the world by shrieking. This resulted in said seagull being challenged by an entire flock for the food that they had so skilfully acquired.

One September afternoon I was sat intently observing a young family eating fish and chips on one of the benches of the Killacourt with a seagull companion patiently standing and waiting alongside me. One of the children kindly threw a chip in my direction. I swiftly picked it up and set off home where I planned to consume it in peace.

My seagull companion took flight and pursued me on my homeward bound journey. Perhaps he considered there could be an opportunity to snatch the food from me? There was no chance I was giving up my chip. I broke in to a quick trot, he too speed up. When I reached my home in Trebarwith Crescent the front door was conveniently open so I darted in. The seagull wisely decided not to follow me indoors.

I enjoyed eating that chip on the floor of the hall. I think it was the most delicious chip I have ever eaten in my life.

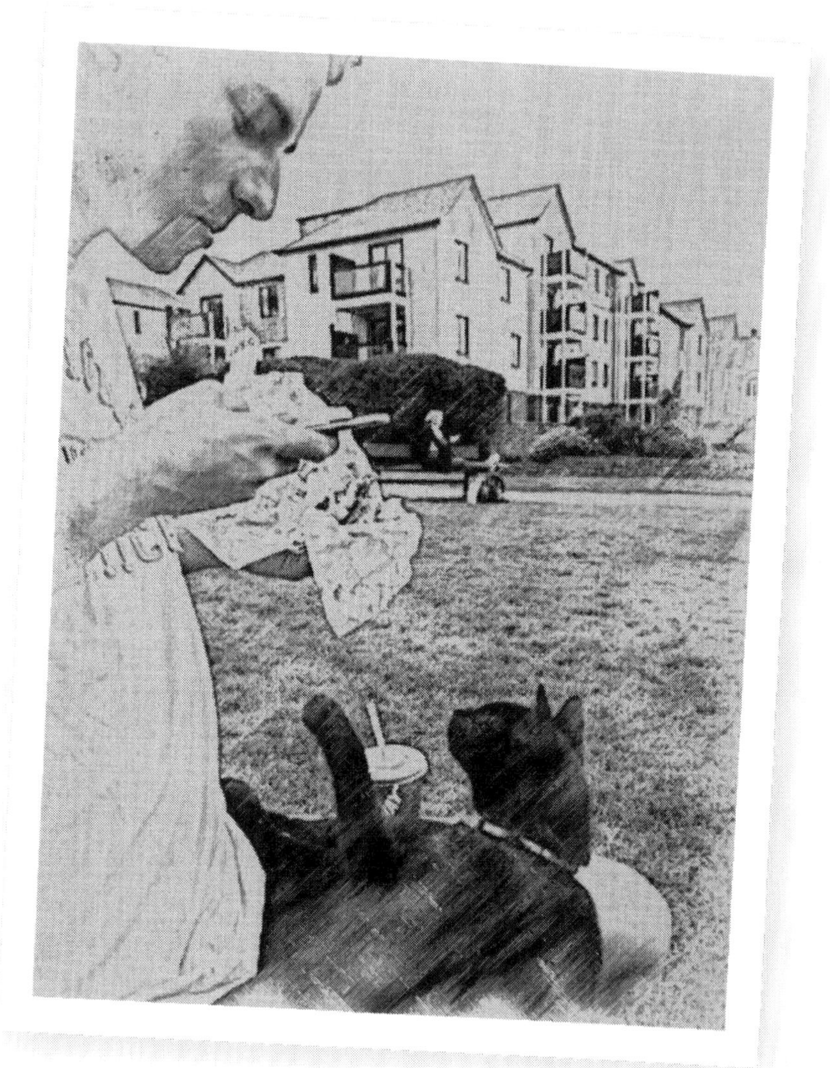

Chapter 20

I'll be there

Craig liked to work in the garage at the back of our house, tinkering under the bonnet of his cars. He was a very practically talented man and when mechanical problems arose on the cars, as they did from time to time, he would have no problem rolling up his sleeves getting his hands dirty and fixing the issue.

Although he was a reasonably accomplished mechanic, he always had been a messy and forgetful man. Rather than have a designated tool box where all his tools that he would need for repairs would be kept, he took to scattering such tools at various random locations all around the house and garage.

The consequence of this was that when it came to needing a specific tool the likelihood would be that he would have no idea where it was and, in reality, little chance of finding it. This meant that fixing was often attempted with the wrong tools making the job much more difficult than it would have been if he had had the right tool.

Craig's mood when attempting any mechanical work in the garage would initially be good but that wouldn't last. As time went on he would get more and more frustrated at the difficulty of his tasks without the use of the correct tools. At some point, there would be the mandatory tool throwing and Craig would eventually revert to shouting curt and unpleasant words with increasing ferocity towards the vehicle he was working on.

I would sometimes go and watch Craig working on the cars in the garage, purely for entertainment purposes.

Oh, oh, I'll be there

When the weather was warm, some local residents took to leaving doors or windows of their homes open. This proved particularly useful to me as I meant I got to explore inside areas that would have otherwise been off limits.

I took advantage of open windows and doors particularly of the houses on Trebarwith Crescent and adjoining Island Crescent.

A lovely couple called Alan and Jan lived on Trebarwith Crescent – just a few doors down from us. They would leave their back door open a lot and, as Jan loved to cook, she would spend a lot of time in her kitchen which was situated at the back of the house.

If I saw their door was open I would climb their steps and walk in. They had a mouthy Jack Russell that lived with them but she was old and almost blind so, although she barked at me a lot, she never really worked out where I was and didn't come near enough to warrant one of my right hook swipes.

I could sit in the kitchen with Jan and Alan for hours whilst they cooked. These were good times; amazing smells with great company. I liked to think I was quite a master of overseeing the food preparation process. Jan and Alan would both regularly provide me with samples of the food they had cooked and I was always vocally complimentary with my critique.

When you need a little love

There were other local properties I visited and spent time including a retirement home on Island Crescent that overlooks the Killacourt. One of the residents that lived on the ground floor would leave her door open every now and then. I would wander in and say, 'Hello' to the elderly lady that resided there. She was always pleased to see me. She greeted me with a lovely warm smile and meek, 'Hello.' After a few visits, she took to keeping some high-quality cat food in her cupboard, which she would offer to me on my visits. Delicious.

I got a little love to share

Next door and the house directly behind our home were two other properties that regularly had ground floor windows or doors open. I mean, honestly, it would almost be rude not to go and investigate.

Next door was very much like our house in the layout and size. Several nice people lived there and when I wandered in from time to time they would all be friendly towards me. One of the residents was called Neil and he was particularly sociable and extremely laid back. He never seemed surprised to see me and would greet me by my name. He smoked a lot and seemed to be almost constantly preparing snacks in the kitchen. Despite my loud demands for him to share, he chose not to.

I would beautifully sing, 'Why don't you feed me? Why don't you feed me?' and his constant reply would be, 'because you don't live here, dude.'

Fair point I suppose, but it didn't deter me from asking again in the future; just in case he had a change of heart.

The open window in the house behind was for a ground floor flat, it was a small collection of rooms of modest size. I think it may have been a holiday let. I did a small amount of washing up with my tongue and then vacated before I could be discovered by whoever the inhabitants might be.

Saturday evenings were pizza night in the Jenkins' house when hot pizza would be brought to the house by a person riding a small motorbike. I enjoyed pizza and every member of the family would share their pizza with me whilst we all sat in the living room. It was lovely family time and my belly was always very full and satisfied on these evenings. Once I had had my fill I would curl up on either Parisa or Craig's lap and sleep off my gorging whilst they enjoyed watching a film together.

I'll be there, I'll be there for you

Although it wasn't the objective, my name tag on my collar ended up working as a kind of un-official tracker and a bit of a personal hindrance. People that I met felt almost compelled to call and check I wasn't lost. These calls to Craig were being made at least once, and sometimes as many as three times day.

In one single day I was collected from Frankie and Benny's, Subway, and then the Killacourt twice (once when sharing ice-cream with two teenage girls and the other whilst fully immersed in a fish and chips fest with friends). Why did people feel it necessary to keep reporting my whereabouts? It was quite annoying.

The calls home reporting my whereabouts hampered my exploring and scavenging missions and definitely messed with my programme. I felt my time wasn't my own and that I didn't have as much freedom as I had been used to. There had to be something I could do to stop this annoyance.

Chapter 21

Uptown funk

I am not sure whether it was an attempt to stop my exploring or cut down the amount of daily phone calls, but Parisa (and sometimes Craig) regularly requested my company in the car which I thought was absolutely fantastic. I got to go in the car to petrol stations, shops, the horses and sometimes here and there for the purpose of human general running around.

Stylin', wilin',

livin' it up in the city

In September 2016 I had my first ride in a convertible car and I have to say that was an incredible experience. I loved it. There is nothing quite like having the wind whistle through your whiskers whilst travelling at speed on an open road in a car with no roof. It was exhilarating and refreshing at the same time.

I do wonder whether Parisa thought that if I went out on trips in the car that it would mean I had less of an urge to go out wandering when I got home. She was, of course, wrong if she thought that.

As soon as I got home from a trip out in the car I would set off out on the streets. It just gave me less time to squeeze in my mandatory scavenging and exploring activities.

October came and I started thinking about exploring further afield. I decided to wander up Marcus Hill, somewhere I hadn't been before. I got about halfway up the middle of the road and sat down to ponder which direction I should set off in next whilst having an impromptu wash. A familiar beeping sound filled the air around me, but, again, I ignored it and just carried on sitting and washing myself, deep in my train of thought.

Stop wait a minute

Less than five minutes later Craig came running up the centre of the road and promptly lifted me up. Apparently, I was causing a road block. Craig took me home and after a bite to eat and a fresh water drink I decided to set off out again. This time I wandered down East Street and onto Bank Street.

Take a sip

It can be actually quite a suntrap down there and I did, from time to time, enjoy sunbathing. Car bonnets, a sunny spot at the top of the Killacourt, and the front garden were my usual sunbathing spots but today there was particularly sunny spot directly outside Costa Coffee so I led down there and proceeded to catch some rays.

I only managed about twenty minutes of sunbathing when two gorgeous ladies walking up Bank Street caught my attention by saying, 'Hello Fudge.' Whilst we were busy having cuddles and conversation Parisa came and collected me. She carried me back home cradled like a baby all the while telling me what a pest I was and how lucky she was to have friends like Caz and Ashe who had informed her of my location.

*B**** say my name you know who I am*

Late one Saturday afternoon I was busy admiring the winter clothing range in the Rip Curl surf shop - just yards from my home. A member of staff cut my shopping experience short by examining my tag and then phoning Craig to ask the mandatory question, 'Have you lost your cat?' Parisa turned up within a few minutes. She picked me and we strolled across the Killacourt taking in the cool sea breeze all the way to The Walkabout restaurant and bar where Craig was waiting for us.

Our mutual friend Richard (the landlord) provided us with a beverage and we all sat happily together appreciating the tremendous view of nothing but the ocean for almost as far as the eye can see.

Saturday night and we in the spot

On 13 October, on one of my many visits to the Killacourt that day I came across a lady snoozing accompanied by her rather placid looking Jack Russell. There was the smell of food emanating from her handbag so I decided to investigate. BINGO! Some crunchy dog biscuits were hibernating in there so I helped myself and munched my way through a few.

This eventually, with the accompaniment of continuous barking from her canine snitch, resulted in her waking. She was surprised but happy to see me, and, realising I was partial to a dog biscuit or two handed me a few more tasty snacks.

She examined the tiresome tag around my neck and consequently phoned Craig to ask if I was lost. At less than fifty yards from home, I definitely wasn't lost. Once she described her location and explained the source of the relentless barking in the background, Craig appeared almost immediately and escorted me home.

I really was getting sick of interruptions of my scavenging and exploring moments. This was simply not on. I'd had enough of everyone cutting my adventures short and it was time to do something about it.

On 16 October 2016 after dinner, I opened the front door with one of my acrobatic moments and disappeared. I wanted time by myself without interruption and that was exactly what I got for six long weeks.

Don't believe me just watch

Chapter 22

Slave to love

On 29 November 2016, Craig and Parisa came and picked me up from the PDSA in Plymouth. Having managed to travel some ninety miles from home I had become unwell and lost quite a lot of weight. I had been handed into the PDSA by someone who had found me wandering on Dartmoor.

Tell her I'll be waiting in the usual place

No one knows how I managed to get to Plymouth or what I did for those six weeks. I didn't even tell Parisa what I got up to, and I tell her virtually everything. It remains a mystery to this day. A bit of mystery is endearing don't you think?

I returned home and began my recovery. I had lots of weight to regain and I was psychologically damaged from my venture. This was my seventh life down.

My recovery was slow. I struggled to be by myself and the times that I did find myself alone I would howl until someone came to comfort me. I had to sleep with Parisa. I curled up beside her in bed at night and she poured love into me.

With the tired and weary

I got walked on the lead again whilst I regained my strength and this went reasonably well. After a few weeks, I was allowed my freedom outside again which also was a struggle. My howling when feeling insecure would now happen outside but fairly quickly my Jenkins' comforter would arrive and take me back to the safety and company of what was the Jenkins' home.

How the strong get weak

It took two months of nurturing but I bounced back to 100 per cent health. Normal business was to resume shortly with food and exploration as my main objectives.

You're running with me

Christmas 2016 was amazing. I have never had eaten so much turkey in my life. It was provided to me on a plate (literally) and I ate like a king with the family at the kitchen table. I feasted until I almost felt like I could burst. The days following Christmas it was fresh turkey and gammon most meal times which again I enjoyed whilst sat at the table.

I will be the same

Eating with the family at the table was now something I partook in three times a day. It ensured I got a varied and luxurious diet. My favourite human meals – other than Christmas turkey – were Paella (I loved prawns and Parisa would kindly remove the shells for me) and Seabass (which Parisa always made sure was safely deboned for me).

At the beginning of January, I had an experience of Tesco's supermarket on East Street as Aaron took me inside with him when he went to buy some milk. It was short-lived visit though as he and I were quietly escorted out of the store by the security guard. Apparently, cats are not allowed in Tesco's.

I can hear your laughter

By mid-January, I was strong and well enough to be allowed outside on my own again for short periods of time. I split my time between outdoor independent time and time with the family with the latter being the predominant.

I started to spend time in the car again and went to various locations running errands with Parisa for purposes mostly connected with caring for her horses. It was great being back in the car.

Whilst on my vacation in Plymouth I had misplaced my name tag from my collar which was, in my opinion, a good thing. It meant I could go about my outside business in Newquay in peace or so I thought. I frequented the usual haunts and a few new places (mainly shops on East Street and Bank Street). My wandering quickly became erratic and busy.

In one day, Craig stumbled upon me in the Fudge shop appreciating the overwhelming smell of sugar and then later on that same day he found me in the back of the Cancer Research Shop where, according to the staff, I was window shopping.

I can see your smile

Following that busy day, I was confined to the house again with car journeys and walks on the lead as my only ventures outside of the four walls of the Jenkins' home. This was ok for a while but I longed for outdoor adventures.

I worked hard to convince the Jenkins' staff to let me out again. I would pace round the house crying (or singing depending on how you look at it) loudly demanding my freedom. As the days, weeks and months passed I increased the intensity of my, 'Let me out now' protests and, by April, they finally conceded and I was allowed back outside on my own. I made the most of it. I had so much I wanted to see and do and time was ticking on.

We're the restless hearted not the chained and bound

I was recognised and greeted by more and more people during my outdoor strolls. Many seemed to know and like me and I think it may have been down to the time I had spent in Plymouth. So many locals had been made aware that I had gone missing and although I was well known before I disappeared, Parisa's efforts to find me (a very public search on Facebook together with hundreds of posters displayed and delivered all around Newquay) meant that my face and name was *almost* famous. I felt like a celebrity.

I enjoyed my newfound status. It's a nice feeling when people know your name without you having to tell them. It made me feel important and respected.

I wasn't spending as much time outdoors on my own as I used to but approximately three hours a day would be my personal requirement and for four months I wasn't interrupted during my local strolling's.

That changed in July co-incidentally when the tourist season started. I was again snapped up by some strangers who saw me walking by the sea front and again considered I was lost. They took me to a vet out of town and for the umpteenth time was collected by Parisa and Craig.

The Jenkins' family saw fit to keep me indoors more during the six-week summer holiday as quite often well-meaning tourists seemed to be insistent on taking me to the vets as either lost or stray. I like to think it's more likely that these people fell in love with me straight away and wanted to have me as their own but all of them (disappointingly for them) were informed by the vets that I already had a family. No one can resist the charms of Fudge Jenkins.

Slave to love

My independent freedom was reinstated for the last time in early September and for one month I was well behaved. It was all a bit boring as all the tourists had left and there were fewer people on the Killacourt and in Newquay generally for me to befriend and acquire food from. I decided it was time to spice things up again.

Chapter 23

Holiday

On 1 October 2017, almost exactly a year from my exploration of Plymouth, I decided I needed another vacation.

If we took a holiday

The first task was to find a suitable mode of transport. Although I enjoyed travelling in cars and wasn't really fussy on which one I should hitchhike in, it seems that some people don't want the company of a cat in their car. My first failed attempt at getting a lift was a taxi.

The taxis that sat at the end of Trebarwith Crescent always seemed to be going on trips. I hopped into one of the stationary taxi's when the door was open and set about making myself comfortable on the back seat. The taxi driver, however, assisted me in a quick exit whilst advising he only took paying customers. As that plan was somewhat foiled. I started looking for an alternative vehicle with a more willing driver. It didn't take me long.

Trebarwith Crescent was, as usual, filled with a warehouse worthy selection of vehicles. I sauntered in and out of the parked cars and stumbled upon the perfect ride; a camper van with its back doors left welcomingly wide open. There was no one in sight so I took the opportunity to hop in and curl up in the back. As I had not long ago had my gourmet breakfast my belly was full and, once I lay down, within a few minutes my heavy eyes had won the battle. It was warm and I soon dozed off. My sleep was deep and considerable.

I was woken some time later by noise and rummaging. I opened my eyes to be greeted with the vision of a kind middle-aged female human with a tinge of sadness in her eyes. I had been sleeping between two suitcases so when she went to move one of them she had disturbed my snooze. The lady was as surprised to see me as I was her. She caringly picked me up and we drove to a vet where she scanned me for a microchip; it was just her and I. Afterwards she took me back to her house – where the van was parked - for safekeeping.

I did not recognise the neighbourhood we were in, we definitely had travelled, but how long the journey had been I really wasn't sure. Her house was nice. It was a similar style and size to my home in Trebarwith Crescent with less mess and less noise. Just two people appeared to reside there as opposed to the noisy Jenkins' clan of animals and humans.

It's time for the good times

I explored the rooms of the house. It was homely and welcoming but, there was an overwhelming feeling of grief in the house, something I had experienced before and didn't enjoy feeling again. I decided that I should leave the inhabitants to deal with their grief privately and looked for the earliest opportunity to vacate the premises.

Forget about the bad times

All the windows and doors in the house, however, appeared shut. I guess this was an effort to keep me safe. I am a cat of inquisitive and persistent nature though so, for a while, I exercised patience and observation. It paid off. Some hours later, a door was, fortunately for me, left ajar and I made a run for it. I was determined to make the most of my annual holiday.

Outside was definitely not Newquay, or Plymouth or, in fact, anywhere I had been before. I found myself to be on a busy wide main road in a residential area. There were large houses on each side set back from the road. Cherry trees lined both sides of the substantial road. It was an area of affluence. The main road was long but that didn't bother me. I was here for a holiday so off exploring I went to see what I could find.

The houses set back from the road were of various styles but they all looked large to me. I took a couple of weeks to explore gardens and meet people and say, 'Hello' in my loud voice. The people were nice and I got attention, some people even fed me but, having been a survivor and an adaptable being I could manage to forage fairly well for myself. I spent the nights sleeping in gardens, as, although it was October, the weather was unusually mild and I didn't feel cold.

As the days and weeks passed I continued to venture along the road all the while looking for food and friends. I came to know that the road I was exploring was called Sandridge Road which is located in the area of St Albans.

I got to know my surroundings pretty well. I stumbled upon a large open green and regularly spent time hanging out there hoping that it might hold the same population and food generosity that the fruitful Killacourt in Newquay offered in the summer months, but, although I did meet a few people there, it wasn't anywhere near as busy as the Newquay.

I had to work quite hard for food but my voice was loud and my will was strong so I managed pretty well, bin foraging was my main source of food. There was a noisy primary school and a pub that I discovered in my wanderings. Children from the school always said, 'Hi' back to me and the outside of the pub had decent sized bins, which were a good source of food.

After about five weeks of wandering the temperature started to drop a little so I decided that my sleeping quarters should now be indoors rather than in the confines of secure gardens under hedges. I found a shed in a garden with a broken wooden panel at the bottom. I managed to negotiate entry by squeezing my slender body through the gap in the wood and started sleeping in there regularly at night. It just meant that if there was rain or it got colder I could stay warm easily.

I was happy with my choice of a vacation destination and got into a good routine of scavenging and making friends in the day and sleeping in my new found shed in the evenings. It was my favourite type of routine.

And bring back all of those happy days

One morning a man came to the shed and disturbed me from my lie in, he was nice and friendly and, as soon as he found me, disappeared back to his house returning with fresh water and food. His waiter type service became daily and took the pressure of my foraging and scavenging efforts. I had found myself a mini cat hotel and felt accomplished in my fortunate discovery.

After about a week of my stay in Catty Hotel, a new lady accompanied my man-servant to the shed one morning. She came with a cat basket – I know what these things are for and happily clambered inside. I meowed asking if we were off to a new destination to extend my holiday experience further but they didn't answer my question. I don't think I was loud enough.

I was taken to the Cats Protection League in St Albans and scanned for a microchip. That was the moment when everyone realised who I was and they were amazed that I had managed to travel 290 miles and survive by myself in St Albans for six weeks. This was my eighth life down.

A phone call was made to Parisa to inform her of my location and I could hear her sob with joy down the phone, 'This is my best birthday ever!'

It's time to celebrate

The date was 15 November 2017 and, unbeknown to me, it happened to be Parisa's fortieth birthday. Apparently, a few days prior to the lady from the Cat's Protection League collecting me, Kayan had suggested that the best birthday present for Parisa would be for me to return home. People could be forgiven for thinking that I had received an invitation to the birthday celebrations and had decided to make an appearance. I hadn't, of course, but it was a happy coincidence.

Let love shine

I was then taken to a foster carers home where I stayed for the next few days whilst transport was sorted to get me back home.

And we will find a way to come together

Whilst in the care of the foster carer I was on the receiving end of what I can only describe as five-star accommodation and treatment. I highly recommend the experience to any animals who are considering it. The Cats Protection League provide a fantastic service. It was like a holiday upgrade without any payment or effort required from me. The foster carer was called Joyce; she fed and watered me and provided me with a litter tray and bed. I wasn't allowed outside, which was a little bit annoying.

Three days later a lady called Sheila came and picked me up (in another cat basket) and transported me in her car to another lady called Louisa from the Charity Last Chance Hotel. Louisa then took me all the way back to Newquay. I highly recommend this charity too; their chauffeur service was faultless.

Just after midnight on 19 November 2017, I arrived home. As Louisa lifted the cat basket out of the car and walked along the road in the darkness I recognised the familiar smells and hustle and bustle of night time Newquay.

And make things better

It was good to be home.

Chapter 24

Celebration

I was handed back to Parisa, who was overjoyed to see me. She was excitedly rambling and kept kissing me, on the top of my head, telling me over and over and over again how pleased she was to see me, how amazing it was that I was home, how difficult it had been to find me and how naughty I was. I didn't really know what all the fuss was about, I'd just been on my annual vacation – no big deal.

Over the next few days, we had lots of visitors at home and it seems I was the star attraction. There had been another huge and successful search for me which had been embarked upon whilst I had been holidaying.

There's a party goin' on right here

Apparently, Parisa had managed to track me down to the St Alban's area - she had been made aware when reporting me as missing to the microchip company that I had been scanned the day after I went missing in St Albans and that I had then escaped from a house in Sandridge Road. This had then resulted in an unbelievable amount of effort being made to find me.

Hundreds of people had joined in the search with people that she didn't even know who lived in the area physically searching and distributing posters.

Parisa who was home in Newquay, 290 miles away, had done everything she could think of remotely to help the search. The local schools and vets had been made aware of me, and radio interviews and newspaper articles had been done. Apparently, I was all over Facebook and the internet as well but obviously, I had been oblivious to all this and been enjoying my new destination without a care in the world.

A photoshoot followed for a local newspaper shortly after my return to Newquay and my adventure to St Albans and back was featured in the local and national press. Some of my fans from Newquay popped in to see me at home tell me how amazing I was.

A celebration to last throughout the years

It seems that what had spurred my journey home was my man-servant who had provided me with food and drink in the shed. He had recognised my picture from a newspaper article in the Herts Advertiser and subsequently contacted the Cats Protection League.

The Jenkins family were glad to have me back but letting me have my freedom outside of the house again was something that didn't happen again. I was only allowed out on supervised walks on the lead. This proved quite entertaining in many ways.

So bring your good times, and your laughter too

The route we would take would not always be the one I would choose and I would object to this by way of a loud growl. It would get the point across but, rarely, would alter the path we would take.

I would be encouraged to toilet outside during my schedule walks but nine times out of ten I would decline. The house environment remained the more convenient and comfortable area to relieve oneself.

My preferred behaviour whilst out on walks would be to roll in the dust on the pavement and generally bimble around rather than go to the toilet. This rolling in the dust on my back would cause whoever my designated Jenkins' walker was (each of the family took it in turns to walk me) to feel embarrassed when people passed us and stared.

Another way of causing embarrassment for my slaves would be when I would adopt the drag pose. This is where I would pick up the pace so that my slave would literally have to run to be able to accompany me. If my human slave failed to accelerate at the same pace as me the pressure of my forward momentum would mean that I would be able to snap the catch on my collar and obtain FREEDOM. This would result in panic from my designated walker and I had found if I then really accelerated away I could get the whole family chasing me down the street screaming my name. Unfortunately, for me, my moment of freedom would be short as they were all quite good at cutting me off but I'm sure it afforded entertainment to any onlookers and, it made my walks more interesting for me.

In order to put an end to my escaping whilst on walks Craig bought a harness for me (I think body cage is a more accurate description). I actually found it quite comfortable but it did spoil my fun a bit. No matter how hard or fast I ran it wouldn't snap open. Damn.

As I was housebound now, I decided that two cat food meals a day were not satisfactory so I started to ask for lunch too. When Parisa came home at lunchtime I would greet her with a very loud version of my, 'I'm starving' song.

It became the routine that I would have three cat food meals a day; breakfast, lunch, and dinner and on top of this I would share all of Parisa's meals with her. I regularly enjoyed eggs, tuna steak, prawns, fillet steak, and seabass. On some days I could also get as many as ten fresh water drinks straight from the tap. I would just sit on the edge of the sink and howl loudly and not stop until someone obliged. The fresh water drinks from various sinks (kitchen and bathroom) were in the morning before and after breakfast, after lunch, after dinner, and sometimes late at night.

It's time to come together

Christmas came around and as was now the tradition, I got my own plate of Christmas dinner. I consumed more turkey than I should have been able to manage and had mountains of cheese as a desert. Good times.

After a while my outside walks became limited to only when the dogs were walked and when the weather was a bad spell, I, more often than not, would decide I didn't want to go outside. As I was perfectly content in the house outside walks for me became obsolete and I was fine with that.

It's up to you, what's your pleasure?

We had a particularly cold spell in April 2018 and snow-covered Newquay. My humans let me out of the front door to inspect it. I hadn't seen snow since our Hawkfield days and I hadn't been outside for some weeks. I went out, as I was allowed to, and had a look and a short saunter but quickly returned to the warm confines of the house. Brrrrrr.

I embraced being a thoroughly spoilt housecat and settled very much into indoor life over the coming months. I slept, ate, and drank lots. I demanded fresh water drinks from the tap whenever I felt thirsty and *reminded* when necessary if I needed more food.

It was essentially a happy retirement for me. I was being well looked after and my needs were met substantially. Gone were the days of wandering and scavenging.

Let's celebrate, it's alright

Chapter 25

One last time

At the beginning of June 2018, I started to feel unwell. My appetite dwindled and I stopped eating. I also stopped talking. Trebarwith Crescent was no longer filled with my dulcet tones; there was no more singing for my breakfast or supper and no loud vocal demands for my fresh water drinks direct from the tap.

On 3 June, after three days of my silent fasting, Parisa took me to the vets as my weight had dropped massively. Whilst in the vets' waiting room an inquisitive and energetic dog bounded in with its owner on tow. Despite feeling extremely poorly, and no longer having much volume to my once piercing voice, I still managed to see him off with an impressive hiss and menacing growl. Parisa quickly apologised to the owner of the dog whilst trying her best to conceal a chuckle under her breath.

I was weighed by the vets and weighed in at six pounds less than half of what had been my body weight in my prime. I was now a physical slither of my previous healthy self.

During my lifetime I had always previously ensured my food intake was generous. My diet had been varied; I had enjoyed freshly hunted wildlife whilst residing in Hawkfield and then takeaway scraps whilst living in Gloucester and then Newquay as well as various types of cat food with gourmet cat food being the preference in my later years as well as luxury human food.

It did seem to Parisa that as soon as the veterinarian heard how old I was the verdict became almost immediately terminal before any tests were carried out, or any treatment was administered.

Blood tests showed that one of my kidneys wasn't functioning well and an X-ray showed a lump on my lungs. There was a suggestion that, given my age and my lack of breathing problems, surgery on the lump on my lungs was not a sensible option.

I was given antibiotic, steroid and B12 injections and also received sedation medication to enable the X-ray to be done effectively.

The vet allowed me to return home with the instruction to the family to continue to try and encourage me to eat and should things not improve I should return to in three to four days. At this time the vet did suggest that, given my tremendous age, euthanasia should be considered.

I was extremely unwell and wobbly when I returned home later on that Monday afternoon, even worse than when I had arrived at the vets early in the morning. I had no food in my belly, you see, and had been overloaded with chemicals which had made me feel even more unwell; not better as we had all hoped.

Parisa turned to Facebook again for help. It had helped when I had been unwell four years previously, it had helped when I had been vacationing in Plymouth and then St Albans, so, maybe, it would help just …

One more time

Parisa asked for friends to send positivity my way as I was very ill. The result of this was that lots of love and lots of advice came pouring in.

A lady called June Jeffrey from St Albans (where I had taken my annual vacation in October 2017) was particularly helpful and knowledgeable. She had, in the past, nursed several elderly cats back to health who had suffered from kidney disease. She told Parisa that it was essential to get me to eat and sent her a link to a helpful website about chronic kidney disease. She also suggested that Parisa get a copy of the blood test results from the vets so that she could decipher exactly what was wrong with me.

Parisa telephoned the vet's and asked to see the blood test results - they were a little reluctant and hesitated but after asking her why she wanted them (where her reply was she wanted to find out what was wrong with me) they emailed them to her and encouraged her to contact them with any questions. Parisa started her own extensive research on kidney disease.

With the help of June and the internet, Parisa started to understand what the blood tests results really meant. There were just three values out of fourteen on the blood test results that were above the normal range; BUN, ALT and AMY. I was likely at stage one of kidney disease. There are three progressively worse stages of kidney disease with stage one being the beginning. It is not entirely impossible to cure kidney disease when it's at an early stage.

June had suggested that I might be feeling nauseous, so, perhaps, an anti-sickness medication such as Cerensa would be a good idea and Parisa was to take this up with the vet.

Parisa purchased some kidney support gold drops for me (a homeopathic herbal remedy) and, at the suggestion of June, some Liquivite cat food which is specialist liquid cat food designed for cats with kidney issues.

The cat food arrived Wednesday just after I had stopped drinking, so, at regular intervals throughout the day, Parisa tried to encourage me to consume the liquidised food. I was less than enthusiastic but, to keep her happy, I did try and stomach small quantities. My intake was, despite my now featherlike body weight, still far below the necessary amount required to sustain my weak body on a long-term basis.

On the morning of Thursday, 6 June (my eighteenth birthday) as I still wasn't drinking anything or eating much at all, Parisa took me back to the vets.

As you know travelling in the car had become a favourite past-time of mine since we moved to Newquay but, I found that journey stressful. I cried quietly a few times on the way. Parisa could feel my distress and tried to comfort me with her soothing soft tone.

This second visit to the vets resulted in Parisa bombarding the resident vet with questions. We could all sense his discomfort under Parisa's interrogation. He didn't enjoy being questioned and pressed at all.

He agreed that it was likely I was suffering from kidney disease but also now thought that I may have some form of cancer. He said that the lump on my lungs was probably secondary and that there may be more lumps internally in my lower body.

Parisa asked if I could be given some anti-sickness medication and, after initially advising they don't normally administer that drug unless vomiting is present, he did agree to give me some, along with further antibiotic and B12 injections. The vet also suggested I be put on a drip for the day as I was now dehydrated as well as grossly underweight.

The dreaded word, 'euthanasia' was mentioned again particularly because I was a cat of great geriatric age.

'Fudge is over a hundred years old in human years,' the vet barked.

'Yes, I know that, but, we must try and help him get better,' was Parisa's sharp reply.

I spent the day at the vets and at half past four that afternoon Craig and Parisa came and collected me. Supplies of hydration solution and specialist cat food were sent home with us this time.

The vet had his most sympathetic face on when we left and told us to see how I coped and bring me back on Saturday should things not improve. The car journey from the vet's to home was the last car journey of my life and I hated it. I was distressed and cried all the way home with my shallow voice. I'd had another harrowing day of being prodded and poked at the vets and, just like the previous vet visit, it had made me feel far worse.

Parisa set about trying to help me as much as she could. At least four times a day she attempted to get me to eat and drink something, and, although I did try, I consumed and drank very little. All I wanted to do was rest my heavy head and my weary body.

A lovely lady called Sarah Everett came to me on Friday afternoon and gave me some hands-on Reiki healing, it was emotionally comforting but my bodily problems were, this time, not to be cured.

Saturday was another day and, according to the vet, when the medication that I had had on Thursday would wear off. I didn't deteriorate though- if anything when the medication wore off I felt a little better. I was still tired and lacking in energy but not so dreadfully unwell. Parisa continued to nurse me around the clock and almost constantly encouraged me to eat and drink. I heard her and Craig discussing the trips I had had to the vets that week, 'We are not taking him back there ever again,' they agreed and I was relieved to hear that.

Sunday was a better day, instead of spending virtually the whole day led out on the kitchen bench, I got up and started to wander around. On Sunday evening I was reasonably bright. I even hauled myself up to the kitchen sink and insisted on a drink of fresh water, something I hadn't done for some days.

The whole of the Jenkins family celebrated that night; this was turning the corner. I was brighter, I was up and about, I was on the mend, or so they thought.

I ate reasonably well that evening and interacted with the family on a minimal level but it was read by all of them as progress and, for the first time in seven days, instead of sorrow, desperation and anxiety, a sense of happiness and relief filled the house.

Parisa was up at 3 a.m. on Monday morning, as she had been for every day for the previous week, to check on me. Every night for the past few days she had left the hob light on for me in the kitchen. The light on the hob reflected off the wooden worktops and created an orange soft light. I had the privilege of a beautiful orange gentle nightlight through the dark hours; it was like a constant sunset. As she opened the kitchen door that morning to tend to me I looked closely at her through the warming orange glow. The effort this human slave had put in for me since she entered my life some eight years ago was insurmountable and it had built to an absolute maximum in the last seven days.

She gives you everything

In front of me stood a physically and emotionally exhausted woman, but, despite this, there was absolutely no way that she would give up on me. I had no doubt her efforts to try and fix me would continue for an indefinite period; she had the energy to do whatever it took to get me well. She desperately wanted to save me and was devoted and selfless in her efforts.

I took my small amount of liquid cat food from her and then would wait quietly for her to return at 7.30 a.m. with more food and water. That feeding session, too, was minimal but I felt she was pleased with the effort I had put into consuming something, no matter how meagre. Parisa would return again later, around midday I expected, as had become the routine.

I spent the morning on the kitchen bench; I didn't get up, I didn't ask for a drink, I didn't make a sound. I just lay there quietly whilst Craig was busy working in the kitchen. He occasionally came over and rubbed the top of my head lovingly and uttered words of affection to me. I tried to smile back but I was tired and felt so very ill. Phoenix my brother from another mother sat next to me all morning. He stared at me the whole time with love in his eyes, he respected me and had grown up learning so many things from me. I felt energy beaming from him, he too was willing me to get up and clout him on the head as I had so often done in the past when he had invaded my space for too long. I couldn't do it though; I had so little physical energy.

At 12.30 p.m. as predicted, Parisa returned and both her and Craig ate their sandwiches sat either side of me. Gone were the days where consuming their food in my company would result in me mugging them and sometimes swiping the food out of their mouths with my claws. Now I couldn't do it, and, honestly, I did not want any more food.

After she had finished her lunch Parisa got my food out and, as she had done many times over the past week, tried to encourage me to take some from her. This time rather than oblige I categorically said, 'NO' with a growl followed by a quiet meow. With as much energy as my body and soul could manage in my weakened state, I walked to the middle section of the kitchen bench (where I used to sit for most of the Jenkins' family meals) and I lay down for one last time.

Parisa and Craig were there by my side and we all knew this was it. Now it was finally time for me to go. Parisa had her hand softly on my rib cage and I felt surrounded by love. It cascaded and poured into me like a waterfall. I could hear her voice but, when I lifted my heavy head and looked up at her, her lips weren't moving, 'It's ok, you can go now. I know you want to and that you need to. I will miss you dreadfully but I understand. Everything will be fine.'

Right there and then at 12.52 p.m. on Monday, 11 June 2018 I took my final breath with both Craig and Parisa by my side. I said goodbye knowing that everyone would be ok and that it was, after an epic eighteen years, the end of my time on this earth.

This was my time to fly having had the most amazing life full of adventures and wonderful experiences. I'd finally used up all of my nine cat lives.

A silent moment followed.

Stay with me a minute

The floods of tears and sobbing then started. Parisa carefully lifted up my limp lifeless body and cradled me like she had done so many times over the past eight years of my life. She held me like a new-born baby and Craig commented how it looked like I was still alive but, obviously, that wasn't true. I'd left my body moments before and was watching from above.

Kayan who was off school that day with gastroenteritis was called down from his bedroom and told it was time to say goodbye to Fudge.

With tears streaming down his face Craig purposely dug a grave for me in the front garden and I was carefully laid to rest. I was placed curled up in a comfortable looking sleeping pose. It was a quiet burial with silent tears pouring down faces.

It was a sad moment but looking down on that scene I could see that I was resting not far from one of my most favourite spots. I had, previously on many occasions, loved to sunbathe in the front garden. It was a lovely sun trap and a fitting place for my final slumber. I was outside where I loved to be without being too far away from the place where I truly belonged and had come to call my best ever home.

One last time I need to be the one to take you home

Chapter 26

(I've had) the time of my life

This is my final chapter - yes, I know - I didn't want it to end either. I've loved sharing my adventures with you but the thing is this is a typical story in that it has to have a beginning, a middle and an end, and rather sadly, this is the end.

I hope you have enjoyed reading about my life as much as I have enjoyed writing about it. It's been amazing, it's been crazy, it's been unbelievable at times but if there is one thing I can categorically say it's that it has constantly been filled with love.

From the moment I entered the Jenkins' home, I was adored and lashings of love have continued to be sent my way for the whole of my life by many, many people. I've lived like a king and the majority of people who have had made my acquaintance couldn't help but grow to love me. Let's face it I'm irresistible, I'm adorable (perhaps a little guilty of being a bit vain) but I have enjoyed the attention that my wicked personality has afforded me.

Thank you for taking the time to hear my story. I can hand on heart say there won't ever be another Fudge Jenkins and, do you know what, that's absolutely fine. My unique personality makes me one in a million and everyone who met me agreed that I am, and I was, a remarkable cat who happened to have a remarkable life.

As a final point I feel I must say thanks to my human slaves (all of them) as, without you, I wouldn't have lived such a wonderfully privileged and adventurous life.

I've had the time of my life

Epilogue

A quarter past midnight

So that was The Adventures of Fudge Jenkins and it's been an absolute pleasure to write it with Fudge as the worthy narrator. I started writing this book in 2015 and it's taken me nearly four years to complete. It's involved hours and hours of careful crafting to enable it be as close to perfection as possible. I always strive for perfection.

The majority of my writing has been in the middle of the night as for, some reason, that's when I feel most inspired.

It's a quarter past midnight
but we are just getting going

Life moves actually pretty fast and we all just seem to keep moving forward even when, perhaps, we should be stopping and appreciating what's around us at the present moment.

Keep on running,
running through a red light

I'm definitely guilty of trying to keep up with the frantic pace of life.

Why are we always chasing after something, trying to throw our lives away?

At times I've found it hard to make time for my writing and, as wonderful as Fudge was, and as brilliant as his life has been until we lost him I think we did underestimate what an exceptional being he was.

We never knew what we had

Fudges' death hit me really hard. I don't think I can really put into words how much I miss him (and I don't think that will ever change). This is not the first time I have experienced great loss.

I wrote twelve skeleton chapters whilst Fudge was alive, sporadically, over a period of three and a half years. When he died it catapulted me back into finishing his book. I filled out the first twelve chapters and wrote fourteen more chapters in just three months. Hopefully, that gives an idea of the enormity of emotion losing him created. Fudge lives on in his book and writing those last chapters made me feel that he was still sauntering around, very much still with me.

I did worry when returning to writing that I wouldn't do him justice, that I'd miss out vital details because, clearly, eighteen years is a long-time and, how on earth could I accurately and realistically recall everything in his life over such a vast period of time? Sometimes I can't even remember what I had for breakfast yesterday, so, initially, I felt there was little hope for long-term memory recall.

I've done it though and it's been mostly by myself although there have been others (mainly my husband and three children) who have helped by relaying their memories of Fudge to me.

It's been an enjoyable but emotional experience. I've relived chapters as I've been writing them with a mixture of feelings.

During most of my writing time, I've felt like Fudge has been curled up on my lap. He certainly was for most of the first three and a half years of writing and I regularly smoothed his soft silky head whilst I was contemplating how to effectively phrase things, and, what words to use. He's been inspirational in his own special way.

This is my favourite part; help me piece it all together darling, before it falls apart, help me piece it all together

If reading this book has made you feel something then I would like to think I have written it well. My aim has always been to write honestly and from the heart which I have found difficult. It's not always easy to express emotions and feelings in words but I've tried my absolute best to do it properly for Fudge. This is, after all, his legacy: a chronicle of his life and time.

A piece of my heart will, for eternity, always be devoted to Fudge. He was, and is, an absolute legend and, I stand by my reflective thoughts.

We never know what we had

Appendix

This section contains all the blogs I ever wrote about Fudge together with the images that accompanied them followed by some photos of Fudge just being his awesome self.

It serves as a reminder of some of his incredible adventures and the impact he had on my life.

My advice to all is take photos and videos of as many happy moments of your life as you practically can because, although that moment passes, you can relive them again and again if you have a recording of it. I constantly relive my great memories of Fudge in this way.

Appendix 1

The miracle that is Fudge Jenkins

Written 23 March 2015

Shortly after getting Bella back my elderly Siamese cat, Fudge, fell ill; he stopped eating and was not drinking at all, had horrendous runny poo and was dribbling from his mouth (almost foaming). This persisted for three days and on the third day I took him to the vets as an emergency (the vets are not open on Sundays so they had to call an emergency vet for me).

I was told after a quick examination - which involved listening to his heart, feeling his stomach and taking his temperature -he most likely had a tummy bug. The vet gave me some probiotic paste and told me to administer it three times a day and syringe water into his mouth. We went home. Fudge was desperate to go back outside when we got back but we didn't let him out. He howled all night long and then the following morning we let him out. Less than 30 minutes later we had a call from the vets (he is microchipped). He had been picked up by someone who was concerned for his welfare and taken him to the vets. I went and picked him up and brought him home and carried on with the treatment.

He stayed in but was very unhappy and at 3am the following morning we let him out because we could not stand the howling all night long again. At around 4pm that day we had a call from the vets, this time the RSPCA had picked him up and taken him to the vets. The vets said they were concerned for him and of course I was too and reminded them that

I had already been to them for a diagnosis and was in the process of administering the paste as instructed but, had noticed he hadn't really improved much at all. They said they were to carry out some blood tests.

An hour later I got the dreaded phone call, I was informed he had acute pancreatitis, was massively dehydrated and had possible kidney or liver failure. The vet told me there was nothing they could do and Fudge needed to be put to sleep. This was hard to swallow but I said I would come and be with him for his last moments.

There was objection to this by the vet but I insisted and eventually he agreed. Craig my husband was desperately upset 'I can't come in with you' he said with tears in his eyes 'I know' I said, understandingly. Fudge has been in his life longer than me. He was Craig's pet with his late wife. The drive to the vets is normally a five minute drive but the traffic was horrendous and it took 25 minutes that night to travel less than 2 miles. During that time, I decided to put Fudge's fate to question, I asked myself (without emotion and objectively) whether it was Fudge's time to go. I was fully prepared for the answer to be yes. You see the experience losing Bella has taught me how to detach myself from my emotions, I believe I wouldn't have been able to speak to Bella telepathically when she was lost if I hadn't mastered detachment from my emotions. Anyway, I asked the question and the reply was 'No it's not his time.' I was surprised by the answer so asked the question again, I got the same answer several times over.

When I arrived at the vets I was ushered in and the vet had the needle ready. I bravely and strongly (I am neither of those things) said, 'I would like to know what the options are and then I will make an educated decision.' The vet looked taken aback. 'There are no options, he will not recover.' I had to push really hard and even ended up asking him what would the treatment be if Fudge was human and I was told there would be nothing they could do, he would suffer a little longer and then die. The vet was very insistent that the kindest thing was to put him to sleep. I, however, said I wasn't prepared to not try and help him, I told the vet I wouldn't be able to live with myself if I didn't try to help our long-standing family friend of 15 years and if he wouldn't try I would look at alternative treatment such as homeopathic methods. He reluctantly agreed to put Fudge on a drip, and that is exactly what happened.

After two days he was well enough to come home. I went to the spiritualist church on the Monday night and, appropriately (and not because I asked), healing was taught. I immediately then started to give Fudge healing. I also put a plea on my Facebook page for people to send positive and healing thoughts to Fudge which many of my lovely members did for me.

Two weeks later I registered him at a new vets and took him for a health check. I told the new vet the history and she said, apart from him being underweight he was healthy and well. Fudge has made a full recovery and now sleeps beside me everynight in bed curled up by my head- he never did this before he was ill. Craig has told me several times how brave I was to question the vet and insist that we try and help Fudge as he said, he would never have had the courage to question the professional verdict.

I am very clear on the fact that if it had been left up to the vet and Craig Fudge would have left our lives last October but thankfully he is still very much a massive part of our lives. He has regained his weight is healthy again and very much a massive personality and presence in our family. I am glad I trusted my instinct on this occasion. I was convinced it wasn't his time to go as much as I knew that Bella was very much alive when she was missing that was what kept me relentlessly searching for her. X

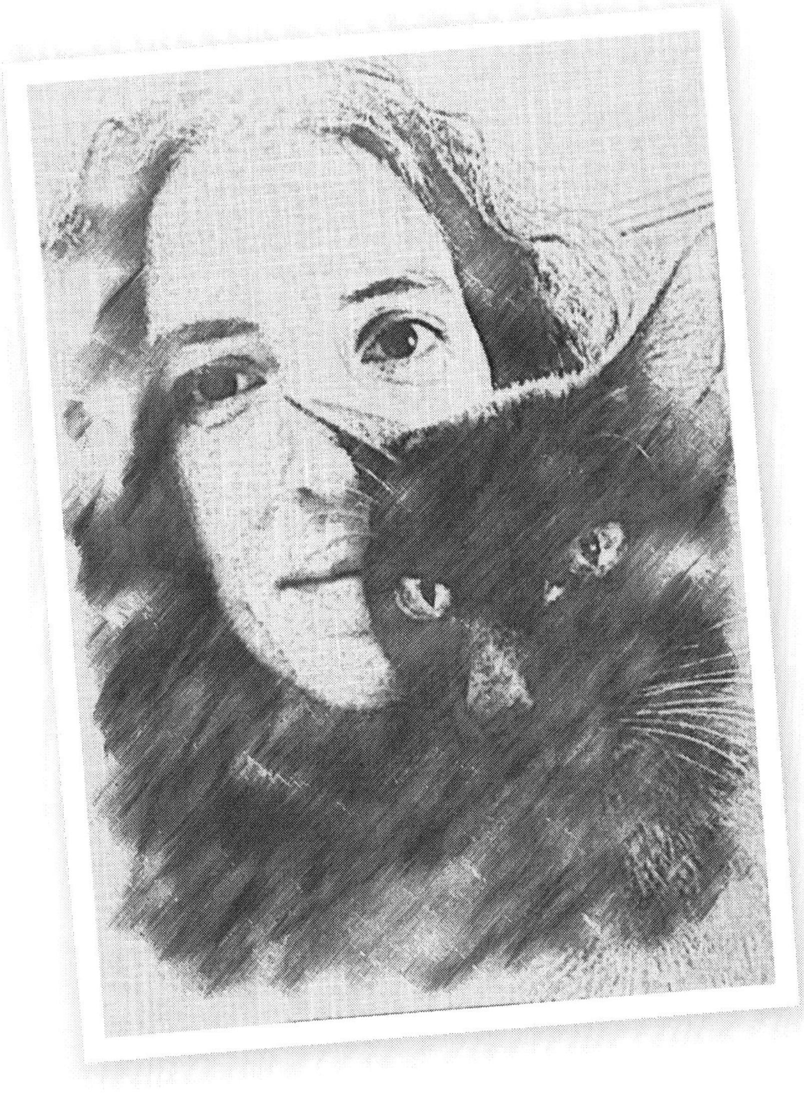

Appendix 2

Nothing will change my love for you

Written 26 October 2016

Fudge is lost and it's almost unbearable.
It seems no matter what I do the message just isn't getting through.
You need to come home Fudge.
Even if the odds are out, even if the words run out, even if the times are tough, nothing will ever change my love for him.
I will spend as long as necessary looking for Fudge, just as I did when Bella was missing.
I like to believe that the message from him is 'I'm coming home to you.'
I truly hope you know, Fudge, that whatever happens, nothing will ever change my love for you.
He's an absolute legend.

Appendix 3

The Greatest

Written 1 November 2016

There is absolutely no question, as far as I am concerned, that Fudge is the greatest cat alive that I have ever known.

Arguably everyone considers their cat the greatest but, let me tell you the reasons why I consider Fudge Jenkins is worthy of such a title and then you can decide for yourself.

He loves a journey in the car, he loves to walk with the dogs on the beach, he loves a visit to the pub for some good old pub grub, he loves to accompany me at the horses, he loves to follow us into town, he loves to scavenge in the bins and bring back scraps for his two fellow housebound catty friends, he loves cuddles, he loves kisses, he loves to open the front door and let himself in and out, he loves to visit local shops, he loves to hang out with friends on the Killacourt, he loves to loiter on the taxi rank on Trebarwith Crescent.

This is just a small insight into the life of Fudge which is a constant and continuous adventure. He will continue to be 'the greatest' in my mind which is why I am not ready to give up and I won't give up in my search for him. I got stamina.

Come home Fudge, I have a book to finish writing about your great adventures and I really don't feel I can do it without you by my side encouraging me. X

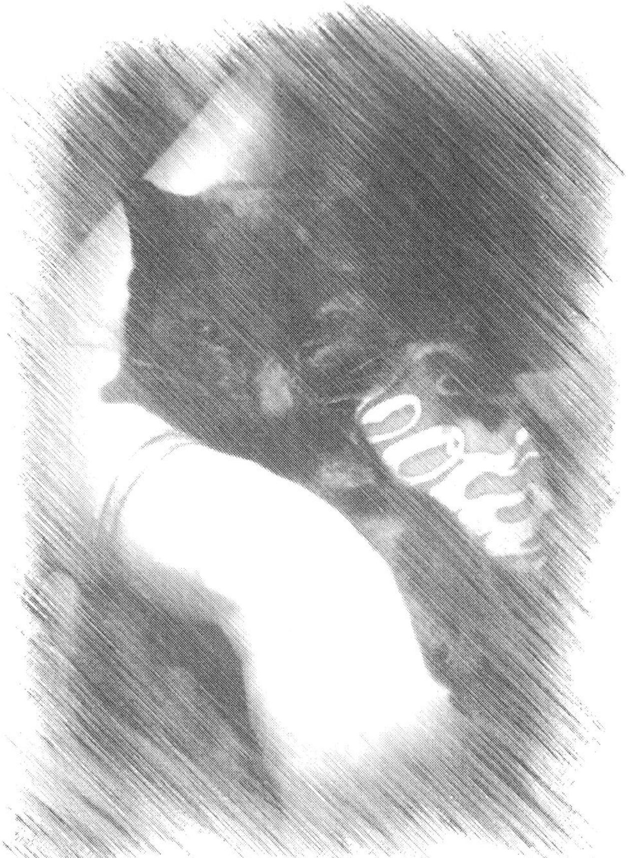

Appendix 4

Starboy

Written on 30 November 2016

The search for Fudge has made him into a star. He already had a fan base because (those who know him will agree) he really is quite a remarkable cat and has an established reputation locally but, now he really is famous.

His picture has been everywhere social media, local press, shop windows, lampposts. So many joined in to try and reunite him with his family that love him more than words can say.

He's been in our children's' lives for as long as they can remember and, of course, he's been in my lovely husband's life longer than I have. It was such a desperate thing to have him lost. I'm crying now, with happiness.

I can't thank people enough for all the positivity, love, support and help that they have poured into the situation. All of the family have struggled the six weeks he has been missing - I actually blame the stress for having not been really well for a while but, surprisingly, I feel almost 100% better today.

I'm so grateful to be welcoming back our little star boy. The family hasn't been the same without you Fudge.

Welcome home my beautiful friend. X

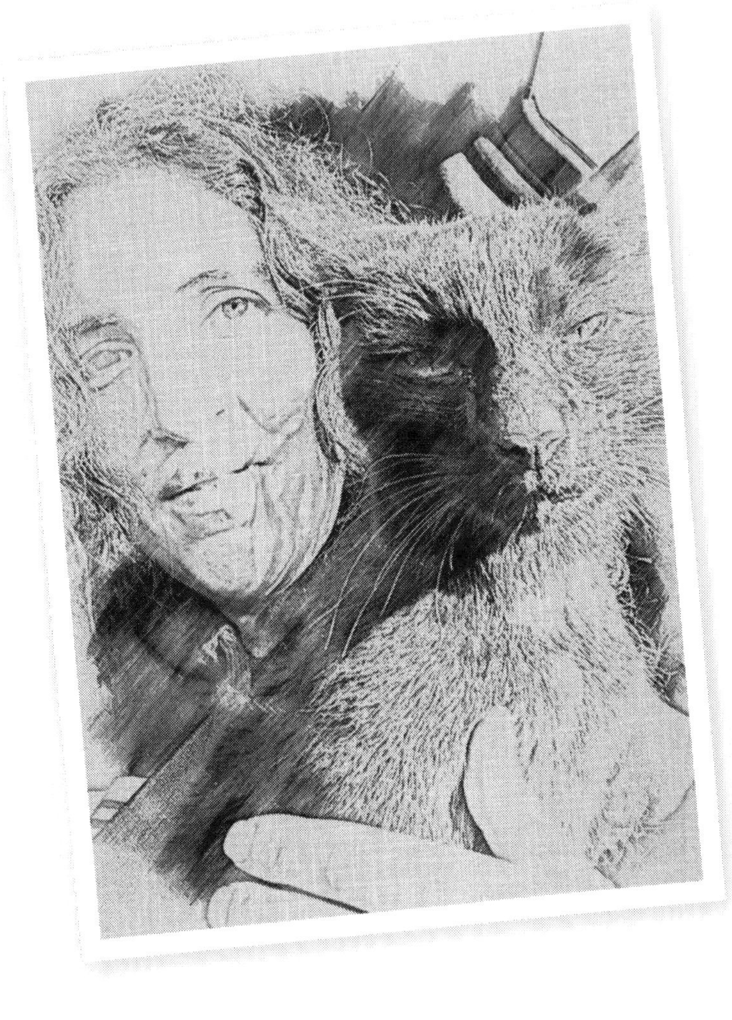

Appendix 5

Find me

Written 1 December 2016

As many of you who follow me as an author know, music is a huge part of my life. Most of the hundreds of blogs I have written have either song titles or lyrics as their titles.

Music inspires me and helps me massively on a daily basis.

When my dog Bella went missing two years ago many inspiration current pop songs helped me through the experience and the same is true for the recent experience of losing and then finding our dear treasured cat, Fudge.

'Starboy' and 'The Greatest' both inspired me to write about Fudge. Also, the song 'Find Me' by Sigma was a song that I seemed to hear a lot when he was missing and, my God, I was trying so hard to find him.

Of course, it was a miracle to find Bella after eight weeks of being missing a mere 230 miles away from home but there has, of course, been another miracle given to me; that of actually finding Fudge.

That song 'Find Me' helped me whilst Fudge was missing. It kept telling me not to give up and gave me hope that I would one day find him. I just didn't know when.

I am so grateful of the messages that are sent to me through music. I consider them magical, inspirational messages in times of need.

Music, for me, is really the soundtrack of my life and I'm blessed to have that, as well as many other wonderful things, in my life.

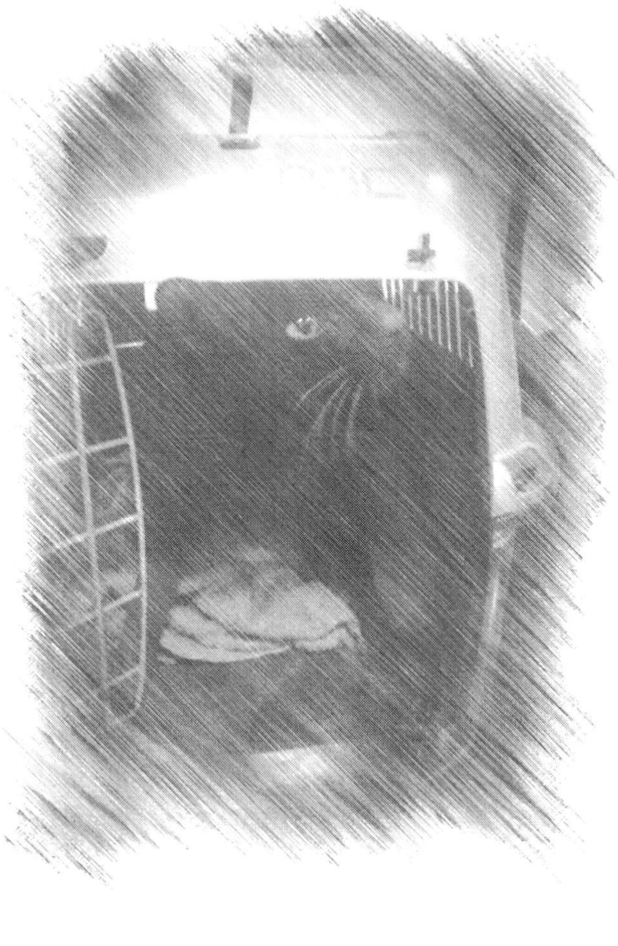

Appendix 6

I miss you

Written 7 November 2017

I know you are somewhere hanging with someone.
I'm wishing that I was your bottle so that I could be close to you again.
Did you not want to tell them it's the end?
I know we are not supposed to talk, but I'm getting ahead of myself. I'm scared when we're not, because I'm scared you are with someone else.
So I guess that you are gone. I just keep finding myself, oh I can't believe it.
I miss you, yeah I miss you, I miss you yeah I miss you, oh I do, though I'm trying not to right now.
You weren't a fan of pictures so I hardly ever took them. Got them saved in my mind. Just to remind myself of how good it is, or was.
I miss you, I'm trying not to right now but I can't help it.
Please come home Fudge Jenkins.

Appendix 7

Facebook

This is the post I wrote on Facebook the day after Fudge came home after his vacation in St Albans (written 16 November 2017).

I can't tell you all how happy and grateful I am.

The residents of St Albans have been utterly amazing and I'm still in shock to be honest about the brilliant outcome.

It's hard to lose a pet, I should know having been through it before, not just with Fudge, but my dog Bella before that. It's even more difficult when you know your pet is lost somewhere more than 200 miles away. How do you practically search when you are that far away?

Well the answer is that there are incredible people in the world, and, when you reach out your hand, vulnerably, and desperately say, 'Please, can you help me?' those incredible people step forward and not only say, 'Yes' but then go above and beyond in their voluntary duty.

I had an incredible fortieth birthday yesterday; a beach ride with two great friends, a surprise lunch with my husband and more brilliant friends and, then, to top it off, the phone call that brought happy tears, informing me that my beloved Fudge is safe and waiting for me to bring him home after his unplanned 6 week vacation in St Albans.

Thank you, thank you. Especially to all my new friends in St Albans and all the amazing people who have offered so much help and support during this trying time.

I am tearfully humbled, honestly.

Appendix 8

No words

Written on 23rd November 2017

What I love about the media attention following the discovery of finding Fudge in St Albans, is that people can't help but show what they are; good or bad.

Following the unintentional act of someone taking Fudge home (that's standard) many people in St Albans and on Facebook have made fantastic efforts to find him. I will be forever grateful for their selfless efforts which have resulted in bringing him back to me. The kindness of strangers has been immense.

On the other side of the coin, according to some 'not so kind' strangers, I am an animal abuser and a very physically unattractive women. No wonder Fudge ran away, apparently.

I've been on the receiving end of internet abuse.

I don't want to sort it out. I keep a small circle of friends; if you are in it then I love you and trust you unconditionally.

These 'trolls' don't know me.

For those that don't know me I can say hand on heart I don't abuse any of my animals.

I can't, unfortunately, change how I look, and, despite the fact I have been reminded of how people think I look unattractive since I was a little girl, I don't want to.

My husband, my kids, my animals, my true friends all love me just the way I am. I will never be Mrs Fantastic.

Having been overwhelmed by human kindness whilst Fudge was missing I've since been reminded of how awful humans can be.

Man are all average.

I don't want to hear no more words from the unhappy and unkind people but I've had no choice.

Thankfully the good people massively outweigh the bad, it still hurts though when people are horrid and it's totally undeserving, but that's the human race for you. There are always rotters but the angels make their presence more bearable.

Appendix 9

I guess I'll wait another lifetime

Written 27 July 2018

I miss you every day. I really do, I think I will feel that way forever.
Your life was more than perfect
How I wish perfect was enough for my own heart.
I thought you'd be with us forever. I really wished that.
Everybody makes mistakes.
I definitely made a mistake on that front. No one lives forever, unfortunately.
The question is....
Do we live and learn to brave them?
I'm always learning - everyday of my life I'm learning and some of those lessons I don't enjoy one bit.
I guess I'll wait another lifetime....to see you again.

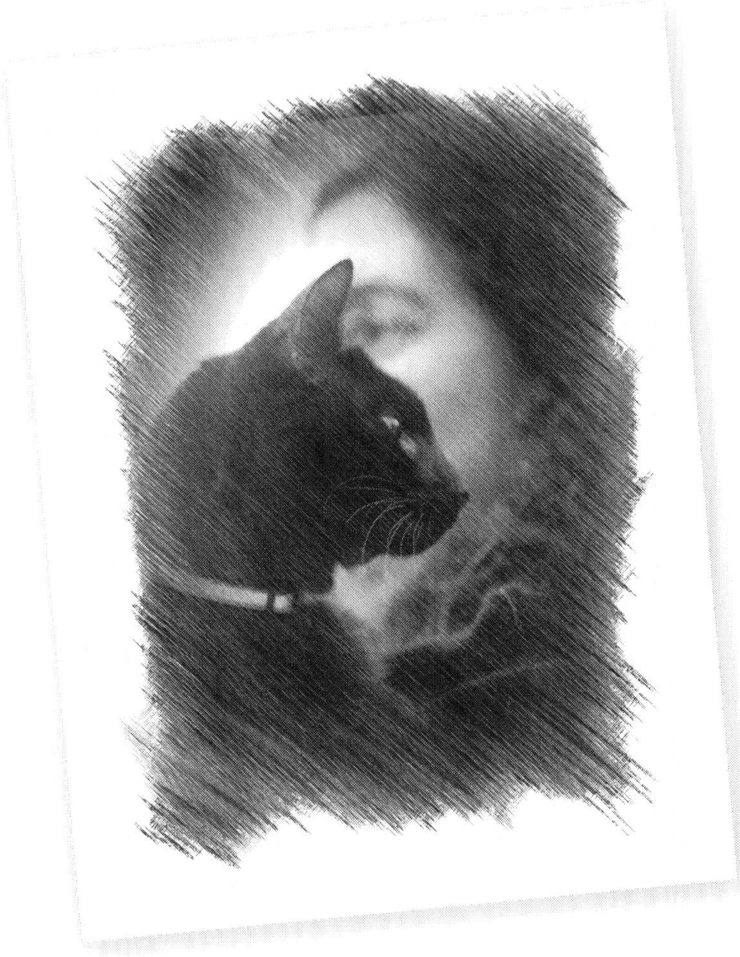

Additional photos

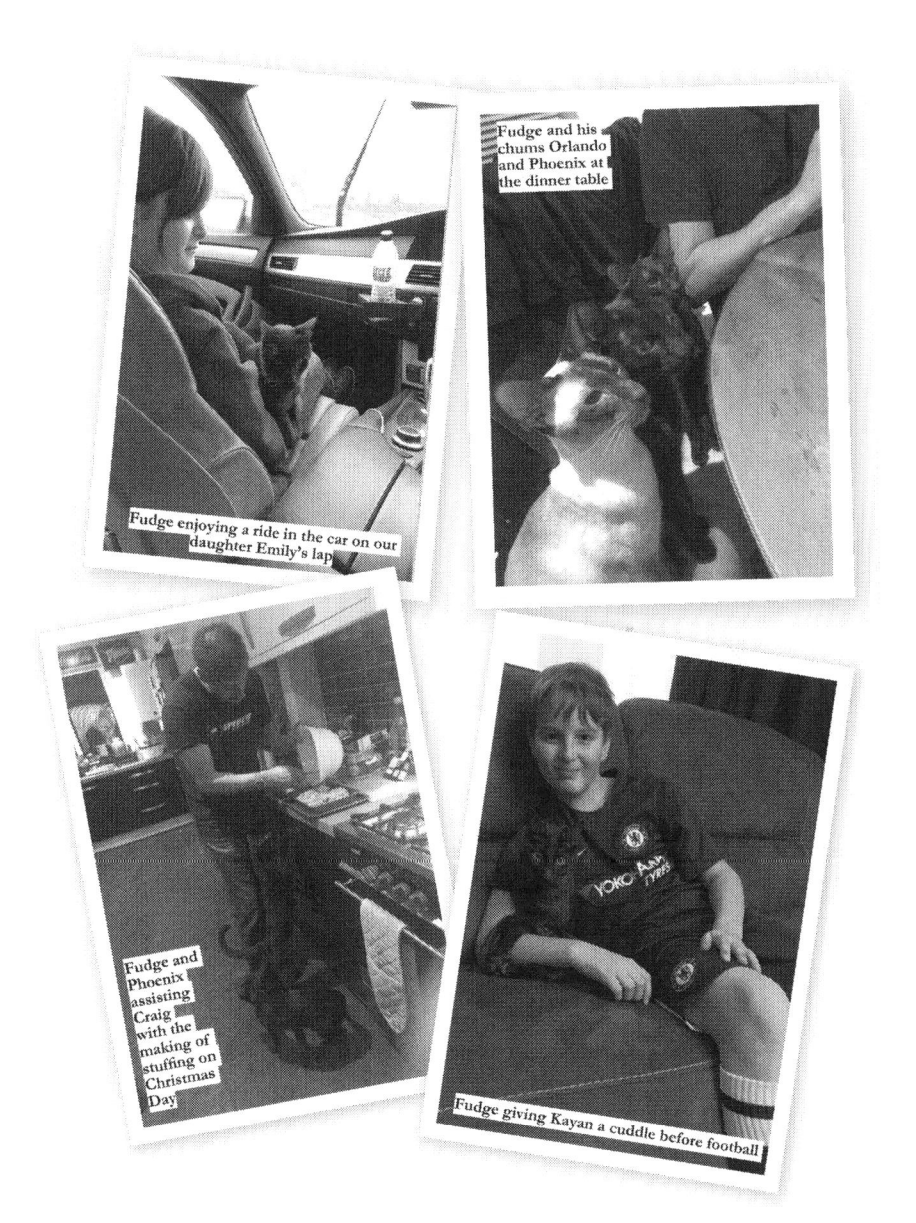

Fudge enjoying a ride in the car on our daughter Emily's lap

Fudge and his chums Orlando and Phoenix at the dinner table

Fudge and Phoenix assisting Craig with the making of stuffing on Christmas Day

Fudge giving Kayan a cuddle before football

Fudge enjoying the view from one of the benches on the Killacourt

Lexi and Fudge queueing for the barbeque.

Fudge helping Aaron eat his dinner

Fudge having 'reluctant' sleeping time with Phoenix and Orlando

Fudge having some relaxing time in the horses field

Fudge travelling in the car.

Fudge spending time on the beach

Fudge and his brother from another mother, Phoenix

Fudge waiting for me in the car at the horses

Fudge enjoying being cradled like a baby

Fudge opening the front door

Fudge on the Killacourt

Fudge taking it all in his stride at the horses

Fudge enjoying a walk on Towan beach

Song titles

Finally, for those who are interested, here is a list of all the song titles and artists that have been used for each of the chapter titles:

Born this way - Lady Gaga
We are family - Sister Sledge
So Good to Me - Chris Malinchak
Broken - Maclean
Let her Go – Passenger
Youngblood – 5 Seconds of Summer
Loves Changes Everything – Climie Fisher
Anywhere – Passenger
Harder Better Faster Stronger – Daft Punk
Open Season – Josef Salvat
High Hopes – Panic at the Disco
King of my Castle – Chris Brann
Express Yourself - Labrinth
Better Together – Jack Johnson
Walking with Elephants – Ten Walls
Magic – Coldplay
Nothing's gonna stop us now - Starship
Lovely day – Bill Withers
Everywhere – Fleetwood Mac
I'll be There – Jess Glynne
Uptown Funk – Bruno Mars and Mark Ronson
Slave to Love – Bryan Ferry
Holiday - Madonna
Celebration – Kool and the gang
One Last Time – Arianna Grande
(I've had) The Time of My Life – Bill Medley and Jennifer Warnes
A quarter past midnight – Bastille

Thank you for reading my book

I hope you have enjoyed it.

Lots of love

Parisa and Fudge Jenkins

x

Printed in Great Britain
by Amazon